D1190152

Change the World with Service Learning

Change the World with Service Learning

How to Organize, Lead, and Assess Service-Learning Projects

Katy Farber

ROWMAN & LITTLEFIELD EDUCATION

A division of

ROWMAN & LITTLEFIELD PUBLISHERS, INC.
Lanham • New York • Toronto • Plymouth, UK

Published by Rowman & Littlefield Education
A division of Rowman & Littlefield Publishers, Inc.
A wholly owned subsidiary of The Rowman & Littlefield Publishing Group, Inc.
4501 Forbes Boulevard, Suite 200, Lanham, Maryland 20706
http://www.rowmaneducation.com

Estover Road, Plymouth PL6 7PY, United Kingdom

British Library Cataloguing in Publication Information Available

Library of Congress Cataloging-in-Publication Data

Farber, Katy.
Change the world with service learning : how to organize, lead, and assess service-learning projects / Katy Farber.
     p. cm.
   Includes bibliographical references.
   ISBN 978-1-60709-695-5 (cloth : alk. paper) — ISBN 978-1-60709-696-2 (pbk. : alk. paper) — ISBN 978-1-60709-697-9 (electronic)
   1. Service learning. 2. Project method in teaching. I. Title.
   LC220.5.F37 2011
   361.3'7—dc20   2010038725

Printed in the United States of America

To my brother, Mike, for always encouraging and believing in me.

Contents

Preface

This book is a guide to help new and experienced teachers across the country make the leap into creating and leading service-learning projects with their students. Many teachers are already doing this meaningful and important work. I hope that if you are, you find ways to deepen, further explore, or assist in your work by reading this book. If you are just starting out with service learning, I hope this book will provide you with relevant information, from teacher to teacher, to make service learning doable in your busy teaching life. This book is for new teachers, experienced teachers, and teachers in non-traditional settings, and it can be used in public and private schools, grades 3–12, and across all subject areas.

Change the World with Service Learning is not a philosophical book filled with educational jargon. It is a guide with parts of the service-learning process, separated into chapters. These topics are the ones that seemed the most useful to me, after practicing service learning with my students for over 10 years.

The title of this book may seem lofty, but by engaging in service learning with your students, you are doing nothing less than changing the world for the better. By letting your students explore and begin to solve real-life problems, they acquire deeper knowledge, new skills, newfound motivation, responsibility, and engagement. The data support this, but the real joy is seeing this happen with your own students.

In chapter 1, service learning is defined and contrasted with community service. Often these concepts are confused, and clarification and definitions help to demonstrate what service learning is all about. Chapter 2 focuses on the many benefits of service learning, which are wide reaching, ranging from academic to social to personal.

Chapter 3 will guide you to gather ideas with your students for service-learning projects in your content area and grade levels. A process for guiding your students, from brainstorming to a focused question, is part of this chapter as well. In chapter 4, teachers will learn to create a plan for the entire service-learning experience. Partnering with the community during service-learning projects is the topic for chapter 5.

Teachers know that working in teams can yield wonderful learning experiences but it can also be a challenge. Chapter 6 will explore how a team might progress through a service-learning project, and troubleshoot challenging or difficult situations. How to assess service-learning projects is the focus of chapter 7. Many examples of rubrics, checklists, and alternative assessments are shared in this chapter. Chapter 8 will show how to develop reflection activities for students to deepen and enrich the service-learning experience.

Funding is a challenge for everyone these days, especially schools. Chapter 9 will explore resources for how to fund your service-learning projects in straightforward and manageable ways. Finally, chapter 10 shares four interviews with creative and dynamic teachers who are currently leading service-learning projects with their classes. Many tips, ideas, and rays of inspiration are to be found in these interviews.

At the end of every chapter, there is a resource section. There is a great wealth of information on the web and in print about service learning. These sections will point you to the most valuable ones within a certain topic. Also, most chapters include an appendix with ready-to-use (or adapt to your needs) teaching resources for service-learning projects. These are meant to be immediately useful for teachers.

On the whole, I hope *Change the World with Service Learning* provides teachers with a relevant, realistic, integrated, and inspirational guide for how to lead service-learning projects with students. Feel free to adapt, adjust, and use whatever you can from this book to help you change the world with service learning!

Acknowledgments

I want to thank Martin Kemple of Foodworks and community member John Puleio for first encouraging me to use service learning as a teaching tool many years ago. From these two I learned how to lead these kinds of projects, and how to connect with the community in meaningful ways. I also want to thank special educator Julie Smart and Farm to School Organizer for Shelburne Farms Dana Hudson for their stellar editing, which went well beyond the bounds of normal friendship. And a big thank you to my students at Rumney Memorial School, who taught me the power and beauty of service learning. They give me hope for the future.

Growing World Changers

Our future leaders
will need to solve
vexing problems
finding sustainable energy
ending hunger
how to live peacefully
stop disease
heal food systems
grow habitats
and more than
I could name
In one poem

What makes us think
that listening
and doing worksheets
will create people
who can save the world?

They need to question
They need to plan
They need to argue
They need to rehearse
and then they need to call
leaders and experts

Themselves

They need to debate
to analyze
and finally decide
what to do
and then do it

Now

They need to see connections
opposing perspectives
listen with grace and respect
but then counter argue
and make their point
eloquently
with examples
from history

We become not
teachers on a stage
but facilitators
mediators
cheerleaders
truth seekers
questioners
reflection makers
and joyful learners

Witnesses
of hope
potential
and our future

This is education
This is teaching
This is learning
That makes a difference

and changes the world

—Katy Farber

About the Author

Katy Farber is a fifth- and sixth-grade teacher at Rumney Memorial School in Middlesex, Vermont. Prior to that, she taught fifth grade at Twinfield Union School, and environmental education at the Taconic Outdoor Education Center in Cold Spring, New York. She has a master's degree in teaching, with a specialization in science, grades seven through nine, from the State University of New York at Plattsburgh.

Katy has served as a teacher mentor, service-learning consultant, and teacher leader in her district. A documentary film by Noodlehead Network called *Is This Going to Be on the Test? Place-Based Learning: Kids Exploring Their Own Community* was created about the service-learning projects completed by her students in 2002. Katy wrote a teacher's guide to accompany this film. She is also a contributor to the book *Reading to Learn, a Classroom Guide to Reading Strategy Instruction*, published by the Vermont Strategic Reading Initiative and the Vermont Department of Education in 2004.

In the fall of 2009, Katy received an Earthwatch Educator Fellowship to participate in a 10-day science research expedition to Louisiana to survey swamps and cypress forests for the effects of climate change and extreme weather. She had the opportunity to communicate with her students via blog posts and Internet video, thus engaging them in real-life science research and field-based learning.

Katy's first book, *Why Great Teachers Quit and How We Can Stop the Exodus*, was published in July 2010 by Corwin Press. She led a workshop on teacher attrition at the National Staff Development Council's Summer Conference for Teacher Leaders and the Administrators Who Support Them, held in Seattle in July 2010.

Katy lives in Vermont with her husband and two daughters.

Introduction

Be the change you wish to see in the world.

—Gandhi

My entry into service learning was not easy or peaceful. When asked what teacher would be crazy enough to lead 50 fifth- and sixth-grade students in a service-learning project that would be videotaped and made into a film for teachers and students, my principal said, "Katy Farber." So there I was, leading students in brainstorming questions about our local watershed, with a microphone on my shirt and a video camera shining a light in my face.

I had led smaller service-learning projects before and had some successes and many challenges. It was after several years of different kids, projects, problems, assessments, community partners, and mentors that I truly felt comfortable with this kind of untraditional, innovative learning.

I have always been idealistic about teaching, thinking that small groups of people could change the world, make a difference, and foster deep learning along the way. This is what service learning does. It turns students into problem solvers, critical thinkers, experimenters—not just receptacles for our knowledge.

My students have located and preserved habitats, built community gardens, set up all-school composting and recycling programs, created numerous field guides, written and illustrated children's books with science themes, and created and performed plays to teach younger students about science, history, and culture. Did they learn what the district, state, and nation say they had to? You bet, and so much more. They learned that they matter in the world, that they can cause change, ask questions, solve problems, get help, and work together to make a difference in their school, community, and the world.

1

This book is a guide for busy, hardworking teachers to start using service learning as a teaching tool, or to extend and enrich what they are already doing. The book is also for environmental educators, child-care providers, after-school program providers, and others interested in pursuing innovative, life-changing service-learning projects with youth. It is my hope that you find it clear, concise, easy to use, motivating, and disarming as you plan your units and lessons in any subject. Service learning has energized my teaching, and it is my hope that it will for you, too. There are many student and societal benefits in service learning that you will read about, but one benefit that is often overlooked is how it can change the way you look at teaching. Witnessing children learning this way gives me hope for the future. Watch your students teach, shine, explore, ask, lead, change, discover, and, eventually, change the world for the better. You will feel the difference.

Chapter 1

What Is Service Learning?

Talk does not cook rice.

—Chinese proverb

Service learning is not a new idea. Teachers across the country, for most of the nineteenth century, have been linking the needs of the community with learning in their classrooms. In fact, John Dewey was a fervent early supporter of service learning. He "believed that students would learn more effectively and become better citizens if they engaged in service to the community and had this service incorporated into their academic curriculum" (NCES, 2010). And that was in 1916! He was way ahead of his time in this (and many other) areas.

So we can see the early roots of service learning, but it did not really gain educational traction until the 1970s. Cognitive psychologists such as Lev Vygotsky and Jerome Bruner pointed out that "learning involves the creation of meaning and is highly individualized," and that service learning provides an opportunity for developing relevant and meaningful ways to learn about abstract and often challenging concepts (USC, 2010). Then, in the 1990s, legislation and support for service learning blossomed.

In the years of 1990–1999, many reforms to support and extend community based learning were put in place, such as The National and Community Service Act of 1990, through the Serve America program, and the National and Community Service Trust Act of 1993, through the Learn and Serve America program, provided support for service-learning activities in elementary and secondary schools (Corporation for National Service, 1999). In addition, through programs such as AmeriCorps, the federal government has offered opportunities to high

3

school graduates, college students, and recent college graduates to serve local communities in exchange for stipends and payment of education loans or money toward future postsecondary education. Both Learn and Serve America and AmeriCorps are administered by the Corporation for National Service, a federal organization also created by the National and Community Service Trust Act of 1993. (NCES, 2010)

Throughout the 2000s, we saw growth in service learning across the country, with some states requiring it for all students.

For half a century, service-learning has spread in American schools. In the last decade, it was spurred to new growth by congressional and presidential actions and funding. In increasing numbers, schools have provided service-learning opportunities for students that connect their curriculum studies to activities such as tutoring younger children, adopting a river, creating a museum exhibit, or conducting oral histories with senior citizens. In these and similar instructional activities, youth have simultaneously learned to serve and served to learn. They are becoming both better students and better citizens. (National Commission on Service Learning, 2010)

With the election of Barack Obama in 2008, a renewed sense of service has been infused in the spirit of our nation and citizenry. With all the development of service-oriented activities in the classroom, there has been a growth of interest in community service and service learning in classroom settings. But there have also been lots of misunderstanding as to what is meant by these terms and how they might ultimately benefit students the most.

If you ask a teacher or parent what service learning is, you'll probably hear them say, "Oh, community service? Our school does that. We have a food drive every year."

While this is wonderful, it is not service learning. There is a lot of confusion about what it really is, and how it is much more than community service. Service learning is not meant to take the place of community service projects that schools are involved in. And it is not simply calling community service by a new name. Community service is extremely valuable and important to schools, communities, families, and individuals. But there are many meaningful differences between the two concepts.

COMMUNITY SERVICE

Let's start by looking at community service. Traditionally community service targets a local or global need or raises money for a cause. The cause and event are usually chosen and led by adults, with support from students and families.

The beneficiary could be a neighbor or the Amazon rain forest, thousands of miles away. Usually this is a finite event, taking up a day, weekend, or few weeks.

Examples of community service are

- food drives, or other collections for charity;
- hospital visits;
- UNICEF or other non-profit support;
- nursing-home visits;
- animal shelter visits;
- cleaning a park or habitat;
- picking up litter;
- helping out at a local library; and
- assisting children or people with learning or physical disabilities.

Community service often benefits a local community, non-profit organization, or group in need. It is practiced by people to connect to and volunteer in their local communities; to fulfill school, business, or extracurricular requirements; or, at times, as a punishment.

Community service may be mandatory, part of a community or court process, or part of a graduation requirement. It generally does not include specific learning objectives or organized reflection and extension opportunities. Community service activities can be a single event, a short series of events, or regular engagement completed in schools, community groups, or clubs.

You have experienced these before and have a good sense of what community service is and looks like. These activities are meaningful and valuable, are usually led and coordinated by adults, and are finite in duration.

HOW SERVICE LEARNING IS DIFFERENT

Service learning is a learning tool to empower students to solve problems in their own communities, or even globally. It is a student-driven process, where students learn about a particular issue, place, or problem, then figure out how to take action in a positive way. Then they actually do it. Students themselves (with teacher guidance) do research, make calls, write letters, and solve problems. Ultimately they share this process with their schools, families, and communities, and that is where the real change happens.

Service learning takes time. It cannot be an add-on to a curriculum. It has to be embedded and integrated for it to work with busy teachers and a full curriculum. Service learning is all about the process: it builds in reflection, takes weeks or months, and culminates in a community celebration. Community service is a piece of this process. In short, community service is "the action" in isolation.

According to Learn and Serve America's National Service Learning Clearinghouse, "Service-Learning is a teaching and learning strategy that integrates meaningful community service with instruction and reflection to enrich the learning experience, teach civic responsibility, and strengthen communities" (NSLC, 2010).

A service-learning non-profit group called KIDS Consortium supplies professional development, grants, and resources to teachers completing service-learning projects with their classes. Their definition of service learning is as follows: "A method of teaching/learning that challenges students to identify, research, propose, and implement solutions to real needs in their school community as part of their curriculum" (KIDS Consortium, 2003).

So while there is crossover, and a definite need for both community service and service learning, there are real and distinct differences. This book is about how to lead, plan, organize, and assess meaningful service-learning projects with your students. Teachers will find that service learning enriches, extends, and enlivens community service in great measure.

This quote sums up the difference between the two concepts:

We define community service as volunteering in the community for some form of extrinsic reward, such as fulfilling a graduation requirement or obtaining class credit. Service learning, in contrast, is a teaching method that combines academic content with direct service experiences in which students provide genuine service to their school or community while extending or deepening their understanding of curricular content. (Hopkins, 2008)

SCHOOLS LOOKING TO CONNECT MORE WITH COMMUNITIES

More and more schools across America now have some sort of service as a regular part of the school experience. According to the National Center of Education Statistics, "sixty-four percent of all public schools, including 83 percent of public high schools, had students participating in community service activities recognized by and/or arranged through the school; [and] fifty-seven percent of all public schools organized community service activities for their students."

For these schools, community service is already happening and with some training and planning, more service learning could take place that would net even more positive results for student and the community. Learning could be extended in rich and meaningful ways by developing service-learning projects in these schools.

Schools are interested in developing problem-solving and critical-thinking students who can handle the challenges of our rapidly changing society.

> About one-fifth (19 percent) of schools with service-learning said that one of their top 3 reasons for encouraging student involvement in service-learning were to teach critical thinking and problem solving skills. In addition, 12 percent of schools with service learning said that improving student achievement in core academic courses was one of their most important reasons for encouraging student involvement in service-learning. (NCES, 2010)

Clearly, schools across the United States are using service as a way to help students improve their academic achievement, and as they do, they are discovering benefits in multiple areas of student achievement and success, as you will see in the upcoming chapter.

Specifically, service learning has the following components, many of which community service and community-based learning do not.

- Service learning is connected to the curriculum or will meet curricular goals (including grade level or grade cluster expectations).
- Community contacts and partnerships are created and fostered, exposing children to community members in real and meaningful ways.
- There is significant student choice in the topic area, project design, and focus.
- There is built-in reflection, so students are constantly thinking about their learning and projects.
- Students work in their communities to solve real-life problems.
- Students are assessed throughout the project in numerous ways.

EXAMPLES OF SERVICE-LEARNING PROJECTS

- Rural Vermont fifth and sixth graders studying sustainability search through school trash and discover that students are not recycling. In committees, students research recyclable items, trash, and recycling companies, and work with a local non-profit to secure recycling bins for the school. Then they teach the school community how and what to recycle.
- "Elementary children in Florida studied the consequences of natural disasters. The class designed a kit for families to use to collect their important papers in case of evacuation with a checklist, tips about rescuing pets, and other advice to make a difficult situation easier, which students distributed

to community members" (National Service Learning Clearinghouse, 2010).

• "Middle school students in Pennsylvania learned about the health consequences of poor nutrition and lack of exercise, and then brought their learning to life by conducting health fairs, creating a healthy cookbook, and opening a fresh fruit and vegetable stand for the school and community" (National Service Learning Clearinghouse, 2010).

• New York City elementary students noticed an ugly, abandoned lot near to their school. They fundraised and organized with community groups to develop a community garden space (National Service Learning Clearing-house, 2010).

• In one high school, a fellow classmate died. The school was devastated and put this energy into creating a memory garden for students who passed away. Students worked with the community sponsors and landscape architects to create a beautiful and meaningful space for the community.

Text Box 1.1

Service Learning Is *Not*

• an add-on, another new thing to do in education,
• a one-time volunteer experience,
• only for older students,
• only for science or civics classes, or
• only for middle- and upper-class students.

In conclusion, the following quote demonstrates the difference between service learning and community service with a clear example:

> If school students collect trash out of an urban streambed, they are providing a service to the community as volunteers; a service that is highly valued and important. On the other hand, when school students collect trash from an urban streambed, then analyze what they found and possible sources so they can share the results with residents of the neighborhood along with suggestions for reducing pollution, they are engaging in service-learning. (National Service Learning Clearinghouse, 2010)

The learning is enriched and extended through service learning in ways that it is just not possible with community service. Service learning is not a new idea. It does not have to be an add-on. Every teacher can make service learning work within his or her grade level, content area, and curriculum.

RESOURCES

National Service Learning Clearinghouse, http://www.servicelearning.org/what-service-learning. Great introductory article about service learning; an all-around information-packed website.

"KIDS As Planners: A Guide to Strengthening Students, Schools and Communities through Service Learning." KIDS Consortium Site, http://www.kidsconsortium.org.

The Complete Guide to Learning Through Community Service: Grades K–9, by Lillian S. Stephens. This hands-on guide to implementing service learning provides information on planning projects, including hundreds of across-the-curriculum tie-in activities, sample projects, forms, questionnaires, and more.

Chapter 2

Why Do Service Learning with Your Students?

I hear and I forget. I see and I remember. I do and I understand.

—Chinese proverb

You might be a teacher wondering why you would want to guide students through a process like this when you can just arrange the details for them yourself more quickly and efficiently. Or you might be wondering how this will work in your particular situation and if it would really benefit your students.

The short answer is, it will benefit them—immensely, in myriad ways, and potentially for a very long time.

This chapter will outline some of the many benefits of service learning for all students. The numbers and information here are critically important. Students benefit academically and socially, and in the area of personal and civic responsibility. With 70 percent of schools doing some sort of service learning and community service, the successes seen from engaging in service learning for some students can make all the difference (NCES, 1999).

STANDARDIZED TESTING GAINS

Teachers and schools have been mandated to do standardized testing in schools more than ever. And with No Child Left Behind, labels and funding are attached to schools based on the results of this high-stakes testing. For better (and for worse), this type of testing is here to stay, and it often is considered a measure of success for schools. This is debatable, as far as success goes, but it is our current reality.

So when your disbelieving principal—or the skeptical superintendent or parent—asks you why you want to do service learning, you can proudly say that service learning raises standardized test scores. It also improves potentially more important lifelong skills, such as civic responsibility and engagement, but we will get to those later on in this chapter. You might also want to use the Principal Discussion Guide provided in appendix 2.1.

Individual schools and districts have been studying the effects of service learning on standardized tests. From increased participation and engagement, students are performing better on these state assessments.

> Service-learning helps academic improvement and higher order thinking skills. Research shows that when service-learning is designed in particular ways, students show gains on measures of academic achievement, including standardized tests. The academic benefits of service-learning come when teachers explicitly tie service activities to standards and learning objectives, and when they design instruction that maximizes learning. Service-learning that includes environmental activities often yields student gains in the content areas of math (e.g., measurement and problem solving) and science (e.g. prediction and knowledge of botany) if these knowledge and skill areas are explicitly woven into the experience. In addition to acquisition of core knowledge and skills, some researchers found that many service-learning tasks help students to improve higher order thinking skills such as analysis, problem solving, decision-making, cognitive complexity, and inferential comprehension because they are exposed to relevant tasks that require them to use these types of skills. This benefit can be realized if teachers play an active role in facilitating dialogue and understanding of more complex tasks. (National Service Learning Clearinghouse, 2008)

Two states have found gains in particular curricular areas.

- "The Michigan study also revealed that service-learning students in the fifth grade demonstrated significantly higher test scores on the state assessment than their nonparticipating peers in the areas of writing, total social studies, and three social studies strands: historical perspective, geographic perspective, and inquiry/decision-making. No other statistically significant differences were found. The two aspects of service-learning that were most closely associated with positive results were linkage with curriculum and direct contact with those being served" (Billig, n.d.).
- In Indiana, service-learning experiences improved standardized tests in both third and tenth grade (Morgan, 1999). "Some schools have documented increased student scores on state standardized testing due to their participation in service-learning projects. For example, in Paoli, Indiana, service-learning has been a part of the curriculum since 1994. This year, only four

high school students failed one portion of the ISTEP. Roger Fisher, Assistant Superintendent for Paoli Community School Corporation, attributes the impressive results, in part, to a desire to attend school and learn that is fueled by their participation in service-learning. He estimates that all members of this year's graduating class will have participated in at least one service-learning project. The Education Commission for the States notes that this phenomenon is taking place nation wide" (Morgan, 1999).

According to researchers on the effects of service learning and standardized tests, "It appears that when high-quality service-learning is intentionally tied to academics, participation can make a difference on standardized tests" (Billig, n.d.).

The key to this success is projects that are intentionally linked to the curriculum, deepening and extending knowledge.

More and more, standardized tests, and life in general, are calling on students to solve critical thinking, in-depth, real-life problems. Word problems that have multiple parts and complex, multifaceted solutions can be less overwhelming when students are considering problems within their own communities and regularly in their school's curriculum. Confidence is built from successful experiences, and this translates to more confidence in a test-taking environment.

Alfie Kohn, an educational researcher and author, often talks about the backward approach with "failing schools." When students are not performing well, often schools will go back to basics, drilling students for limited chunks of information, often without much student thinking or logic expected or practiced. Students are also exposed to a more standardized reading curriculum, with a focus on scripted reading programs that a teacher merely follows. Kohn (2002) describes this phenomenon quite well:

Often, of course, they can succeed in raising average test scores. You deprive kids of recess, eliminate music and the arts, cut back the class meetings and discussions of current events, offer less time to read books for pleasure, squeeze out the field trips and interdisciplinary projects and high-quality electives, spend enough time teaching test-taking tricks, and, you bet, it's possible to raise the scores. But that result is meaningless at best. When a school or district reports better test results this year than last, knowledgeable parents and other observers respond by saying, "So what?" (because higher test scores do not necessarily reflect higher quality teaching and learning)—or even, "Uh-oh" (because higher test scores may indicate lower quality teaching and learning).

And once you realize that the tests are unreliable indicators of quality, then what possible reason would there be to subject kids—usually African American and Latino kids—to those mind-numbing, spirit-killing, regimented instructional programs that were designed principally to raise test scores? If your only argument in favor of such a program is that it improves results on deeply flawed tests, you haven't offered any real argument at all. Knock out the artificial supports propping up "Success for All," "Open Court," "Reading Mastery," and other prefabricated exercises in drilling kids to produce right answers (often without any understanding), and these programs will then collapse of their own dead weight.

What then lacks in the setting Kohn describes is the developing ability of students to solve complex and real-life problems. When reforming schools to promote academic success and boost test scores, educational leaders should not simply rely on route memorization, drills, and scripted programs. They should incorporate service learning in equal measure to give students exposure to this type of in-depth, integrated learning. Raising test scores in and of itself is not the answer, as Mr. Kohn points out—it is raising them while developing our students' critical thinking and real-world problem-solving skills.

IMPROVED GPA AND ATTENDANCE

Many studies have linked service learning with improved GPA and attendance records of students. When so many students are disenfranchised and disconnected from schools and learning, service learning can provide meaning and motivation for students to show up and care about their work. This lends itself to more success in all subjects, by increasing attendance and motivation.

This trend seems particularly powerful for students with risk factors against achieving academic success. According to the article "15 Effective Strategies for Improving Student Attendance and Truancy Prevention," by Jay Smink and Mary S. Reimer, "[s]tudies of the effects of service-learning on grades, attendance, and dropout reduction indicate the value of this strategy for students who have significant risk factors" (Shumer and Duckenfield, 2004, p. 156).

There has been significant data to support the effects of improved attendance and GPA on students involved in service learning. Read on for more survey information from Civic Enterprises (Bridgeland, DiIulio, and Wulsin, 2008) that is quite striking in its support of service learning:

The Potential to Increase Student Attendance and Engagement

- 82 percent of students who participate in service-learning, and 80 percent of at-risk students not in service-learning programs, say their feelings about attending high school became or would become more positive as a result of service-learning. In focus groups, teachers highlighted the value of service-learning in increasing school and classroom attendance, and other studies have shown that high quality service-learning programs have a significant impact on student attendance.

- Other research shows that service-learning can help increase students' self-confidence, leadership skills, and sense of empowerment.
- Secondary research shows that service-learning can improve academic performance by improving test scores, homework completion, and grades, and can reduce the achievement gap between minority and majority students. Teachers explained in the focus groups that service-learning especially helps those who are not best served by the traditional classroom environment.
- Other studies also show that service-learning can improve student behavior, refocusing the school environment on learning while reducing the distractions caused by disruptive behavior.

Students find a voice and passion that is not present in "normal" school through service learning. One student said, "Service-learning makes me want to come to school, because it's not the same thing all the time" (Bridgeland, DiIulio, and Wulsin, 2008). Amen to that. Service-learning projects are different day to day, week to week, project to project, based on the student groups, the focus, the teachers and community leaders, and school settings. Students thrive with this real-life, complex problem solving, which more closely resembles the problems and opportunities they will encounter as adults. They show up more, and that is half the battle in improving academic achievement.

REDUCED DROPOUT RATES

Even more than merely showing up and being involved is the idea that students are more likely to stay in school when they are involved in service learning. How powerful this is: service learning can profoundly affect a student's life by impacting his or her decision to stay in school.

Service learning is quickly becoming a learning tool to prevent students from dropping out of school. Again from the report "Engaged for Success: Service Learning as a Tool for Dropout Prevention" (Bridgeland, DiIulio, and Wulsin, 2008):

Making Service-Learning More Widely Available as a Dropout Prevention Tool

Service-learning alone cannot solve the complex problem of high school dropouts, but it can be a powerful tool to help address many of the warning signs that signal students are on track to leave school—absenteeism, lack of motivation, lack of engagement in classroom learning, and lack of connection to real-world opportunities. Students themselves believe service-learning would be a power-ful tool to prevent high school dropout and want more access to service-learning opportunities.

• Seventy-four percent of African Americans, 70 percent of Hispanics, and 64 percent of all students said that service-learning could have a big effect on keeping dropouts in school. More than half of all at-risk students (53%) believed that service-learning could have this effect.
• Eighty-three percent of all students, 90 percent of African Americans, 83 percent of Hispanics, and 81 percent of whites, said they would definitely or probably enroll in service-learning classes if they were offered at their school.

When considering the motivation of young people to stay in school, despite challenges and serious risk factors, one high school dropout put it succinctly in the report *The Silent Epidemic: Perspectives of High School Dropouts*:

One bright young woman who was a leader in her focus group said: "If they related to me more and understand that at that point in time, my life was . . . what I was going through, where I lived, where I came from. Who knows? That book might have been in my book bag. I might have bought a book bag and done some work."

Text Box 2.1

Students are looking for real and meaningful interactions with the world around them. Service learning gives students more reasons to show up, try, and stay in school. The authors of *The Silent Epidemic* shared these recommendations (see below) to decrease the rate of school dropouts in America, and service learning plays a key role in this process.

Recommendations:

1. Researchers should directly examine the relationship between service learning and dropout prevention.
2. The U.S. Department of Education and state departments of education should work to increase access to service learning for every student.
3. Every school district should have a service learning coordinator who helps teachers implement effective programs and who encourages students—especially those at risk of dropping out—to enroll in classes that include service learning.

To help keep students in school and headed toward a brighter, fuller future, these recommendations should be implemented nationwide.

Eighty-one percent of survey respondents said that if schools provided opportunities for real-world learning (internships, service-learning projects, and other opportunities), it would have improved the students' chances of graduating from high school. Outside studies have noted that clarifying the link between schooling and getting a job may convince more students to stay in school (Bridgeland, DiIulio, and Morison, 2006).

CIVIC RESPONSIBILITY

Students who participate in service learning gain knowledge about the world around them and become motivated to change and improve it. They learn about laws, politics, the environment, communities, non-profits, different socioeconomic levels, and it often changes their perspective on the world. Students who participate in service learning have increased feelings of civic responsibility and engagement. This is obviously what we want from our citizens and future voters.

One study of 4,057 students from 52 high schools in Chicago found that they "foster notable improvements in students' commitments to civic participation. Discussing civic and political issues with one's parents, extra-curricular activities other than sports, and living in a civically responsive neighborhood also appear to meaningfully support this goal" (Kahne and Sporte, 2007).

Another study found impressive increases in student levels of civic engagement and responsibility as a result of service learning:

Kahne and Westheimer (2003) used surveys, observations, interviews, and student work to study 10 such programs. In one project, some students spent a semester investigating whether residents in their neighborhood wanted curbside recycling, and others helped develop a five-year plan for the fire and rescue department. All the students collected data from citizens and government agency staff and presented their findings to their county board of supervisors. The researchers found that, compared with a control group, participating students made significantly larger gains in developing such civic skills as vision and community engagement. (David, 2009)

Boston teacher Jeremy Greenfield knows this. He leads service-learning projects that focus on justice in local communities and empower his students.

Learning that justice is not simply a subject in a book, but a day-to-day, life or death matter, students investigate the current state of their own community. Touring a neighborhood initiative and conducting interviews, students begin to explain how justice is served or not served in the community. As local issues and topics arise, the project becomes student-inspired and student-driven. After reading about urban ecology and environmental justice, one student wants to know, "Is my community environmentally safe?" A study of urban poverty and gangs helps another understand why there are so many neighborhood gangs. The culminating Community Justice Career Fair brings information to several classes of peers. By planning and carrying out this event, students learn the intricacies and difficulties of planning community action. Meeting professional community activists connects the classroom experience to careers and demonstrates that Bringing Justice Home [the project name] starts with informed citizens. (Greenfield, n.d.)

Jeremy Greenfield's work might have lasting affects—his students may be more likely to vote, to volunteer, to be informed, and to be leaders in their own communities. To me, a teacher who also uses service learning, this is not surprising at all. Students live and breathe this work—it engages them in ways they might have never experienced before. These new thoughts, new actions, and new connections can yield more informed, active, and responsible future American citizens. And with the problems facing our society today, we definitely need that!

IMPROVEMENTS IN POSITIVE BEHAVIORS AND ATTITUDES

It is clear to me that students involved in service learning have more positive behaviors and attitudes about school. But we do not have to rely on one teacher's anecdotal observations. Now, there is data to support these improvements in students' behavior and attitudes. Billig (2002) outlines recent studies and their results:

About a dozen studies have been conducted over the past three years that have shown the impact of service-learning on students' academic achievement. Two state level studies are of note: In Michigan, students that participated in Learn and Serve–funded programs were compared to matched groups of students who did not participate in service-learning (Billig and Klute, 2003). Researchers compared the students on measures of school engagement and on their performance on the Michigan Educational Assessment Program (MEAP). The study had 1,988 student respondents, 1,437 of whom participated in service-learning. Results showed that service-learning students in grades 7–12 reported more cognitive engagement in English/language arts (e.g., paying more attention to schoolwork, putting forth effort) than nonparticipants. For students in grades 2–5, students who participated in service-learning reported greater levels of behavioral, affective, and cognitive engagement in school than their nonparticipating peers, showing statistically significant differences in the effort they expended, paying attention, completing homework on time, and sharing what they learned with others. The Michigan study also revealed that service-learning students in the fifth grade demonstrated significantly higher test scores on the state assessment than their nonparticipating peers in the areas of writing, total social studies, and three social studies strands: historical perspective, geographic perspective, and inquiry/decision-making.

In a recent article on Edutopia, the many benefits of service learning are highlighted, as well as words from a veteran teacher who started using service learning as a learning tool.

Benefits of service learning: Kids who are excited about what they learn tend to dig more deeply and to expand their interest in learning to a wide array of subjects. They retain what they learn rather than forget it as soon as they disgorge it for a test. They make connections and apply their learning to other problems. They learn how to collaborate, and their social skills improve. They are more confident talking to groups of people, including adults. And, as a number of research reports suggest, project-based learning correlates positively with improved test scores, reduced absenteeism, and fewer disciplinary problems.

"I've seen test scores of students rise because of the engagement in project-based learning," says Gwendolyn Faulkner, former technology coordinator at Harriet Tubman Elementary School, in Washington, DC. "I saw my students mainstream out of English as a Second Language into the mainstream classroom. I saw my mainstream students scoring three and four grades above their grade level on standardized tests. I'm a convert." (Curtis, 2001)

COMMUNITY CONNECTIONS

This chapter has reviewed some current data about the benefits of service learning. But there are many less quantifiable benefits for schools and the community.

Consider the importance of students developing relationships with people outside of the school community. By interviewing local experts, elders, or other community members, students develop relationships and see the opportunities for themselves in a new way. Students who feel noticed, known, and included in their communities can feel more valuable and important. These qualities are sure to develop more confidence and social skills, and to banish some of the isolation that adolescence can cause.

The community can also view the school and students in a different light. Consider a local business owner's change of perspective about teenagers when they are helping community elders, raising funds for a non-profit, or cleaning up a local park. These relationships can break stereotypes and change the perspectives of community leaders about students and the schools. This, in turn, can lead to more support for school budgets, a decrease in crime, and more involvement from the community in schools in real and powerful ways.

This chapter only scratches the surface of how students can benefit from service learning. Clearly, we see improvement in students' achievement, GPA, attendance, sense of civil engagement and responsibility, behavior, and attitudes. The reasons for integrating this powerful learning tool into your teaching are numerous and clear. Read on to learn to integrate your existing goals with service-learning projects.

RESOURCES

A review of current articles linking service learning and reduced dropout rates can be found at http://www.servicelearning.org/instant_info/bibs/k-12_bibs/dropout_prevention/index.php.

A list of resources available from the National Commission on Service Learning can be found at http://www.servicelearning.org/topic/dropout_prevention.

Benefits of Service Learning for students, teachers, parents can be found at http://emedia.leeward.hawaii.edu/servicelearning/benefits.htm.

Service Learning Benefit Fact Sheet, http://www.servicelearning.org/instant_info/fact_sheets/cb_facts/benefits_cbosl.

Practical experience and improved self-esteem among benefits of service learning at http://www.humankinetics.com/excerpts/excerpts/practical-experience-improved-self-esteem-among-benefits-of-service-learning.

Studies that support project-based learning, at http://www.edutopia.org/project-based-learning-research.

Service Learning and Social Responsibility, at http://www.ascd.org/publications/educational_leadership/may09/vol66/num08/Service_Learning_and_Civic_Participation.aspx.

Chapter 3

Gathering Ideas

Good ideas are common— what is uncommon is people who will work hard enough to bring them about.

—Buddha

What teacher does not love the energy and excitement generated when you brainstorm a list of ideas? Students are creative, divergent thinkers who never cease to amaze me with their unique perspectives and ideas. That said, it can be a challenge to help students brainstorm within a particular curricular area and then focus these creative ideas into realistic questions and topics for service learning. This chapter will help you guide your students from wild idea to focused topic in a way that honors student choice and interest, and fosters positive grouping and curricular goals.

DISCOVERING YOUR TOPIC AND CURRICULAR NEEDS

Before you can brainstorm with students, you need to decide what curricular areas you plan on addressing within your district's or school's curriculum. For elementary teachers who teach all academic content areas, decide which subject or subjects you would like to complete a project in (literacy, math, social studies, or science). For middle-school and high-school teachers or specialists, consider within your content area what unit or theme you would like the project to be a part of. Consult your district curriculum or the Grade Level Expectations and Grade Cluster Expectations for standards that need to be addressed, within an academic subject, or as an integrated unit. Service learning does not stick to one content area, so students will explore different academic and real-world subjects as the project progresses, but you can have specific learning goals or standards in mind when you begin.

To see a list of possible project ideas by content area, see appendix 3.0.

Try to identify between 6 and 10 standards, objectives, or curricular goals before you begin the project. These are concepts you need students to understand by the end of the project, and they are expressly linked to (or even quoted from) your school's curriculum or state and national standards. Once you have this list, you can inform parents of these curricular goals before you begin (see appendix 3.1).

When you have these curricular goals outlined, you can either plan lessons to meet these before you begin the project, as prerequisite knowledge, or you can tailor the project to include these concepts. If you choose to have students meet the curricular goals with the project itself, write a series of focused questions that can guide your students. These questions should be open ended, using higher-level thinking skills from Bloom's taxonomy (see appendix 3.2) to guide students into deep critical thinking about a topic.

After you have written a few questions, target the specific areas you would like to focus on. Then include these key components throughout the project, in student assessments, project requirements, and reflections. The more you address these curricular goals, the more likely students will meet or even exceed your expectations. In some of my projects, I have kept the questions very open ended, and followed student interest freely. In others, I focused more on 3–4 concepts. Think about your curricular needs and goals, as well as your philosophy about student learning, as you design these questions.

In appendix 3.3, you will find an example of the guiding questions that I wrote to inspire and motivate students to reflect on what they want to learn and the learning goals I wanted them to achieve. Your guiding questions will be vastly different depending on your topic area. You can also have students list topics instead of questions. The resulting ideas and projects met standards (and went way beyond) in the curricular areas as well as standards I selected.

THE GUIDING QUESTION BRAINSTORM

Now you have your curricular goals and your guiding questions. What next? It is time to bring in the students. Give each student your guiding questions, and give them ample time to brainstorm and answer them fully. They should be able to do it independently, in teams, or in small groups. The goal here is to have the room buzzing with ideas and excitement about the prospect of studying what they want to! This is a liberating and empowering idea that will excite many students.

Students who have been in a more traditional learning environment might need prompting to expand their minds and think creatively. Encourage students to write down all of their ideas without limitation. This is an idea-generating time free from judgment. You can also set out items to help students along in their thinking, such as maps, historical artifacts, field guides, photos, anything that has to do with your topic that might spark some creative thinking. You might also lead this brainstorming activity as a whole class on a Smart board or whiteboard.

Once you have collected the responses (or can look back at the Smart board or whiteboard), and you have some time, sit down on your own and begin listing the consistent themes and topics you see. List all of these, grouping similar ideas into phrases or questions on a master list (see appendix 3.4). You will probably have at least 20 or so topic areas. Type these up, and then get ready to help the students prioritize their interests.

Copy your new student-generated question list for each student. During the next class period, explain that students should number the questions in order of preference from one to five. Five different choices will give you some room for grouping needs and issues. It is essential that students' choices reflect their personal interests, not their friends'. For that reason, it should be a silent, independent activity. Also, students should know that the teacher will seriously consider their preferences, along with many other considerations, such as group dynamics and student abilities and concerns.

THE CRUCIAL TASK: DEVELOPING
SERVICE-LEARNING TEAMS

Now, this task will take some time. Try to set aside a planning period for a thoughtful reflection of student groupings. There are many issues to consider while creating service-learning teams.

First, take a look at the students' selections to get a sense of patterns and popular ideas. Then list out several group titles you feel will be represented (it helps to do this all in pencil, as the list can change frequently). This is not set in stone, and as you sort through student responses you can add or change the teams as needed.

Next, go through the student responses, penciling students into different groups, considering student ability, gender, special needs, and group dynamics. Teams can range from two to four people, a size I have found optimal for service-learning projects. Any more than that and the teamwork seems to break down, especially with upper-elementary and middle-school students.

Text Box 3.1

Gathering Ideas Summary

1. Teacher selects subject area and curricular goals.
2. Teacher creates a few guiding questions for students in a subject area, with the curricular goals in mind.
3. Students answer the guiding questions, coming up with their own questions about a topic (this can be done on paper individually, or on a smart/whiteboard as a class).
4. Teacher collects the student responses and organizes them into project topics (or titles).
5. Teacher starts assigning students to particular topics based on interest, student ability, gender, special needs, and behaviors. Teams of 2–4 students are optimal.

Continue to group students this way, working from the list and from what you know about each child. It is important not to rush this, because often the success of the project is really based on the members of the group and how they work together. If you work in a team of teachers, or you are a new teacher, it would be helpful to ask your colleagues to take a look at your draft of groupings for any ideas or concerns. It is also helpful to touch base with the special educator in your school for feedback about specific student needs in teams.

HELPFUL GROUPING HINTS

- When you group students of different abilities, do not always put one high-achieving student to lead the group. It is not fair that our high-achieving students are always put in this role. Instead, think about pairing students with a similar ability level, or having two students at about the same level and two students at a different level within a group.
- Carefully look at behavioral needs. This is a project with some freedom and independence, and students who are likely to get each other off task should not be together.
- Students with special needs can participate in regular groups but might need specific tasks and support to help achieve group goals.
- Consider the classroom support you may have. Classroom assistants, parent volunteers, and administrators might be available at different times to support teams.

Once your teams are ready, your students are close to beginning their service learning experience! Now it is time to plan for the project using your class schedule, school schedule, and the unit's duration. In chapter 4, "Planning Considerations, Step by Step," we will look at how to plan the whole experience, because timing is crucial to the project's success.

In the appendixes for this chapter are examples from an integrated unit in science and social studies, but they can be adapted to any subject. You will also find a list of project ideas from a variety of subjects in appendix 3.0.

RESOURCES

How to Start a Service Learning Project, at http://www.mcsc.k12.in.us/corp/service/howto.htm.

How to Develop Service Projects, at http://www.learning-for-life.org/exploring/resources/99-720/y05.pdf.

Chapter 4

Planning Considerations,
Step by Step

To accomplish great things, we must not only act, but also dream; not only plan, but also believe.

—Anatole France

Teachers will find that by doing some planning in advance, service-learning projects can be much more enjoyable. By considering the ideas in this chapter—before you begin creating, organizing, and assessing service-learning projects—you can be more comfortable and relaxed throughout the experience (and believe me, I learned this the hard way!). It is beneficial if you do these planning steps either before the student brainstorming outlined in chapter 3, or simultaneously. This will give your team teachers a chance to join you in this work.

SCHEDULES AND TIMING

The first thing you will need to decide is the unit length and time period. Most projects take at least four weeks, working at least one hour per day. This is a very general guideline for upper-elementary and middle-grade students. More time would likely be beneficial for younger students.

Some schools do service learning as an integrated unit, working for two or more hours a day, for several weeks. This format does allow for more depth in the project and potential off-site work.

In some cases, integrated service-learning projects take all day, with all teachers from all academic subjects assisting and encouraging students to reach out beyond one particular academic area. These are often designed by a group of teachers and staff members, and goals are embedded throughout the project in multiple disciplines. For example, a month-long middle-school integrated unit on the environment includes specific content learning, guided by student interest and curricular goals. Then students develop lessons plans to teach to the elementary schools about this topic. Finally, students travel in teams to the various elementary schools and teach these lessons as a service to the community.

Another way to handle the timing of the project is to work backward from the culminating event. Select the most appropriate date for the final event, discussing it with your school's administrative assistant and consulting the school calendar to ensure there are no conflicts. Count backward at least four weeks from that date to determine when to begin the project.

TEAM WITH YOUR PEOPLE
(THE TEACHER TEAM AND PRINCIPAL)

Now that you have your timing worked out, it is time to bring in your team-mates. During your weekly unit meeting (hopefully you have one—if not, schedule a working lunch or meet during a prep period), share the timing for your project with your team teachers. Look for ways you can work together and support the learning in each other's classrooms. If your team teacher is working with you on the project, share the responsibilities such as the other items on this list, or those suggested in chapter 5. Also, your team teachers can help you troubleshoot issues that might not have occurred to you in your planning. It will also help to have them on board because you will ultimately need their support and flexibility (not to mention any random materials a student group might need!).

Meet with your special-education team. Share the curricular goals, schedule, dates, and any assessments you have developed. With service learning, you will get the highest buy-in from all students, special education or not. They will be motivated and will want to contribute. So it is crucial that the special-education team meet to identify students that might need extra support and come up with ways to accommodate the assessment and project to their needs. Any paraprofessionals can be assigned to assist groups with lower-functioning students to ensure stronger teamwork and support.

With service learning, students are often researching, guided by interest and the topic. Special-education students will need support with this level of research and writing. There are ways everyone can be included in service-learning projects. As a team, students work out a timeline and delegate responsibilities. The special-education team can brainstorm specific tasks and responsibilities for students needing lots of educational support and guidance. Meeting with your special-education team will help you get out in front of any issues that might arise and plan to meet the needs of special-education students in a student-led and student-driven project such as this.

Once you have the unit duration, a date for the culminating event, and a date when projects are due, meet with principal, or principals, to discuss how he or she can be supportive. You will probably need funding, volunteers, good press to parents and school boards, and general goodwill for the project. The more organized you can be before this meeting, the better. If you have to, you can point to the measurable amounts of student improvement on standardized test scores for students (see chapter 2 and the talking points in appendix 2.1) who participate in service learning. And you can point out the data that show service learning improves graduation rates, civic responsibility, motivation, and school attendance, just to seal the deal. Often, schools have discretionary funds in small amounts that principals control. You might want to explain that as the project proceeds unforeseen expenses might come up (seeds, plants, poster board, sign-making materials, recycling bins, etc.), and see if you might be able to access alternative funds. If not, there are more ways to secure funding that will be discussed in chapter 9, but this is definitely an area to explore with your principal.

Go out of your way to talk with the custodians, school cook, librarian, and technology support staff about your project. They will be instrumental to your success with these projects. Why?

On any given day during the project you might need to send students to these people to ask questions, do research, get materials, or learn a skill. They will need to be invested and aware of the project so they know students might be coming their way. Also, they might need ideas for how to guide them. Early one-on-one chats with these professionals (particularly the ones you think will be impacted most—for example, projects on local eating might impact the school cook more than the custodian, but planting a garden impacts the school custodian and/or groundskeeper more) can smooth over any potential conflicts and provide more buy-in and support from these parties.

Take a few minutes at a staff meeting to explain what you are doing. At the staff meeting, briefly explain to staff (and support staff) what service learning is, what the focus of this year's project is, what they might see, and how they might be helpful. Then send out an e-mail with the same information. This will head off any potential misunderstandings when students are using the phone to call experts, looking for the custodian for a shovel to begin their herb garden, or congregating outside in a habitat.

In some schools, special passes will be needed, or a procedure for student teams to gain access to resources and space for their work. Adult supervision will be needed for specific projects, and this will need to be worked out in advance (paraprofessionals, parent volunteers, and specials teachers are all good for this role). This will not look like traditional education. Students will be empowered and getting their hands dirty, literally in some cases and figuratively in all cases. This is not easy or quick work.

School staff may notice more freedom and liberty with this project, and they might need some help to understand and support it. Also, by explaining this to all school staff, you see who might be a good resource for your students to assist with such things as materials, support, expertise, guidance, media support, and small-group supervision. Many school staff members will be excited about this project, some will be too busy to care much about it, and some will think it is not education at all. This will vary from school to school. As the school staff sees the engagement, success, and excitement the projects bring to the school, their ideas about this type of learning will change as well.

PLAN THE ASSESSMENT AND NEEDED RESOURCES

Now that you have some dates and a schedule, and support from your fellow teachers and building leader, start planning for the main assessment of the project. I discuss a portfolio system (and provide reproducible materials in the appendix) for this in chapter 8. Use this assessment, or develop your own, featuring the curricular goals you outlined in the last chapter. Rubrics often work well for this. I use a combination of a portfolio and a project rubric.

Consider that in the culminating event, you want students to feature their work through visual, written, and oral forms. By using these three modalities, students can showcase their work in a way that is meaningful to them and have a greater impact because their message will be learned more fully if presented in several different ways. For example, students preserving an amphibian habitat on their school property might perform a skit about the species that live there, show the signage they created to protect the area, and present the group with an amphibian guide to the school campus. That way, they will be sharing their knowledge in a written, visual, and oral way for a greater impact. The assessment can reflect these different modalities.

Next, you will want to brainstorm or locate any potential resources you may need for the project. This might involve help from the community, a process that will be outlined in the next chapter. But start listing your needs now, so you can begin to anticipate areas where you need support, funding, or volunteer donations. That way when the opportunity arises to fulfill a need, you will be ready.

ORGANIZE YOURSELF

If you are anything like me, you have to-do lists all over your desk, and other notes scrawled on sticky notes. With service learning (as with most teaching), the amount of material and paperwork to manage can be overwhelming unless you have a system in place.

Teachers are unique in their systems for organization, but here are a few ideas:

- Set up a binder with all your service-learning plans, brainstorms, schedules, assessments, and contact information. Accordion folders also work well for managing larger amounts.
- You may want to have a folder, or a section of a binder, for each student group. That way you can keep resources, observations, and assessments separate. They are also very easy to find this way.
- Have a file on your computer or server devoted to a year's or semester's service-learning projects. Save all materials in that folder, and hopefully you can find it and use it again next year.
- Save hard copies of everything: assessments, project work, observations, photos, all of it, so you can have a valuable service-learning resource in years to come. This is particularly handy if a computer or server crashes. (Besides, a service-learning project is an impressive project to add to your teaching portfolio.)

PLAN FOR THE CULMINATING EVENT

The big show is important. After all your students' hard work, you really want to showcase their achievements to parents and the whole school community. Thinking out a plan in advance will help you see where you are going and ensure that nothing surprises you (well, not really, this is service learning after all, and it is always surprising!).

Briefly outline a plan for the culminating event. Will it be outside or inside? At what location would you like to have it? Consider how many people you will be inviting (the whole school, a grade, specific grades or groups) and who will actually come (probably about half that number). Who do you have to ask and schedule with? If it is to be in the school cafeteria, you will need to work with custodial and kitchen staff (that is why you had the one-on-one chat earlier!). If it is outside, you might need to coordinate with physical education or other scheduled outdoor activities. Will you need extra tables, chairs, or other materials?

Then, make a list and tuck it away for the days right before the culminating event. Also, make a list of what has to be done in the week and days before the event, such as inviting and scheduling visits from other classes (these usually need to be circulated at least one week in advance). It is good to do this via e-mail with classroom teachers, about one to two weeks in advance. Then teachers can look at their schedules and plan when it is best to visit with their students.

In the week before the event, call your local newspaper to describe the event and ask for a photographer, or e-mail a press release (the good press will support you, your school, and service learning—more on this in the next chapter). Be sure to invite parents in multiple ways: via the all-school newsletter, your classroom newsletter or a class letter, and school website. Parents often need at least a week to change their work schedules to attend events during the school day.

This is what the culminating event might look like: a whiteboard shares the name of the service-learning fair—such as "The Wonders of the Worcester Watershed!"—and gives directions for visitors as to where the students and the projects are located. Students are in their teams, sitting together at stations outside of the school, or in the gymnasium. Their projects are set up on desks, and they have created a presentation about their projects for their particular audience. The school community that was invited visits these student stations for 3–10 minutes each. In small groups, the visitors travel around each student team station to hear all about the amazing service-learning projects the students completed. During this learning fair, the principal wanders to stations too, as do any important community members, the superintendent, invited press, and parents.

PLAN FOR PRETEACHING

Students will likely need some background in the area of focus for the service-learning project. Say you are about to embark on service-learning projects on our current food system. You will need to preteach about the industrial food process currently used in the United States and worldwide, and the growing local and organic food movement. You might want to teach about the global climate change effects of shipping food worldwide, about the ecological effects (and history) of pesticide use, genetically modified food, and other ideas. You might want to have students discover these concepts on their own throughout the project, and plan for this, or you might want them to go into more depth with this prior knowledge.

What has worked for me was to teach the basics of the area of focus—such as ecology, government, journalism, or any topic. Then, use those concepts as a springboard for the project. For your particular level, you might want to do more or less preteaching. It is variable, based on student age, topic, and curricular goals.

Like anything, service learning is improved (and is much more manageable for everyone) with a little planning in these different areas. Take notes as you proceed through your projects or write all over this section of the book, because the considerations you face at your school could be different and more extensive. This ongoing reflection will help you develop your skills as a service-learning facilitator. Next, we will look at how to partner with the community for successful service-learning projects.

RESOURCES

K–12 Service Learning Project Planning Toolkit, at http://www.servicelearning.org/ filemanager/download/8542_K-12_SL_Toolkit_UPDATED.pdf.

Multicultural Service Learning Teacher Planning Sheet, at http://www.tolerance.org/ activity/multicultural-service-learning-teacher-p.

Service Learning: A Guide to Planning, Implementing, and Assessing Student Projects, by Sally Berman.

Chapter 5

Partnering with the Community

Never doubt that a small group of thoughtful, committed citizens can change the world. Indeed, it's the only thing that ever has.

—Margret Mead (1901–1978)

If the saying "It takes a village to raise a child" is true, then the same can be said of service-learning projects. It takes a team of caring, motivated adults to successfully lead a comprehensive service-learning project. Usually, teachers are the self-sufficient type who can handle most classroom challenges, projects, and issues on their own. This is not one of those times. The more community involvement there is in service-learning projects, the more engagement, investment, and empowerment is given to both the students and the community members. Students need all kinds of role models, and service learning can allow students access to people they might never have met before. It is thrilling for students to see people in the community caring about what they are doing and what they have to say. It is also powerful for upper-elementary, middle-, and high-school students to explore different roles and careers in the community. It can seem daunting, especially to a new teacher, to figure out how to find community members and volunteers to help out with the project. What follows are clear strategies with examples for how to find, organize, and use volunteers from the community in your service-learning project. Using parental support in a positive way and gaining administrative support will be reviewed as well. Finally, we will explore how to contact local media to promote your school's service-learning project so the community can celebrate all of your students' (and your!) hard work.

FINDING A COMMUNITY SAGE AND LOCAL EXPERTS

If you live far away from your school, or have limited knowledge about the community in which your school is located, it will be essential that you find a well-connected "community sage." This person ideally will have lived in the community for a long time. It could be the custodian, a fellow teacher or staff member, or maybe a parent of a current or former student. You will need to ask around, talk to people in the teacher's room, and search for information about community resources on the service-learning project's main topics. You could also e-mail your school staff to see if anyone has any resources or information about your class topics. When you hear back from people or you find your community sage, start a contact log. This log will list all of the possible people you could contact (or better yet, students could contact) to help out. If your topic is environmental sustainability, for example, you will want to write down the name and contact information for the Solid Waste Management district office in your area, the nearest recycling center, and any community organizations that have goals of lessening landfill waste. If your community contact knows individuals who are experts in this area, get their contact information. You will not be contacting these people personally, unless you want some background information, or you want to set up a field trip. It will be the students' responsibility to contact each person or organization, with support, as this is an important part of the learning experience. See appendix 5.1, which has a contact log for you and your students to use.

If you cannot find a community sage or need more experts, consider sending home a survey for the parents. At the beginning of the year, I send parents a survey about their hobbies, areas of interest, and the possibility of classroom volunteering (see appendix 5.2). Then, when I am beginning these projects, I pull them out and see who I could have my students contact if they need to. At the same time, you could ask parents if they are interested in volunteering with any other parts of the project. Who knows, you could have a business executive whose hobby is creating maps, birding, or gardening. Parents are a wealth of information that should be utilized in creating a rich educational experience for students.

PARENT SUPPORT: WHAT IT MIGHT
LOOK LIKE, WHAT YOU MIGHT NEED

We all know that parents' ability to help within the classroom varies widely. The last thing you want is a parent you need to constantly guide, which might take away time from your involvement with students. Yet it is almost impossible to complete these projects without considerable support from parents or school staff. It is critical that parents or school staff have a known, clear support role. Here are few ideas that have worked well within my classroom:

Field Trip Supervisor (or Small Group Supervisor): With approval from your administrator, a parent may be able to take a small group to meet with a local expert or to visit a business or organization that can help with the project. Students should have questions, clipboards, and pencils ready. This is a great support, which allows you to be in the classroom with the other groups. Or this person could supervise a small group when an expert visits on site (which might be a safer bet in larger schools with more liability issues).

Materials Organizer: A parent might be able to help track down needed materials, such as water test kits, shovels, fish tanks, or anything you might need.

Photographer: A parent could document each group's work. This could then be used to help assess students, to promote the project, and to document the learning experience.

Media Contact: A parent could contact the local media so the community is informed about the project and has an opportunity to be a part of the celebration at the end of the unit. E-mailing and calling local radio stations, newspapers, and television stations is difficult during a busy teaching day. This is a great way for parents to support service learning and generate positive press for the school.

As you plan for parental involvement, try to give clear roles and goals so the experience will be successful for everyone involved.

ADMINISTRATIVE SUPPORT

Partnering with your principal as you begin a service-learning project will be extremely helpful. This is important because you will potentially need approval and support for any projects that are building- and campus-wide. If the principal is new or has no experience with service learning, share some resources (such as this book!) with him or her so he or she can more fully understand the benefits and process of service learning. As soon as you can, schedule a meeting with your principal before you begin a service-learning project (as discussed in the previous chapter). Provide an overview of the project, list any needed materials and resources, and explain how you see your principal being involved. In most cases, the principal gives approval and guidance about different school projects that will be created by your students.

For example, some of my students wanted to label a wetland area near our playground with signs to protect it from damage. They had to seek approval from the principal, the recreation department, and the custodian. Having an open-door policy also helps with principal communication. Ask your principal to stop by during class when students will be working on the project. This way, the principal will see service learning in action, and he or she will be able to provide leadership and support as needed.

We all know that principals can be insanely busy, so in reality your principal might not stop by at all. In that case, be sure to invite him or her to your culminating celebration. This will do several good things: it will hopefully impress your principal, who will then sing your praises to the community; it will build positive relationships with your students and the principal; and it will educate your principal about service learning in general.

GOOD PR: THE MEDIA!

One thing I have found very true in teaching: no one knows about all the great work you are doing with students unless you tell them. Many teachers do not want to toot their own horn, or seem too full of themselves. The truth is, if you do not publicize your great work in service learning, no one will know you are doing it. More importantly, community involvement is essential to a good project. It is also very helpful for your reputation and career!

You might have several students who need added challenges and who are not overwhelmed with the project. These students can be on the public relations team, and with your support, they can help with the items listed below. This is a great way to motivate your students who love to write and talk with people.

Of course, we are trained teachers, and not PR executives. Here are some simple tips to generate media coverage of your project.

E-mail or call your local paper, and describe the project, or send them a press release (see examples in appendixes 5.3 and 5.4). Share how many students are working on it, what exactly they are doing, what the impact will be, and how the projects will change the world. Newspapers love stories like this. Hopefully they will send out a reporter and photographer to meet with you and your students.

E-mail or call the calendar coordinator at your local paper, and share with him or her the date of the community project celebration. This will be great exposure and increase student motivation.

Call your local community radio station and have them list the community project celebration in their calendar. They might also be interested in interviewing a student on the air. Use one of the members of your student PR team.

E-mail the school staff to schedule visits to your students' stations during the community share. Set up a schedule for visits and put it in the teachers' room or do it online. Encourage the whole school to come out and view your students' amazing work.

Send home an invitation to parents about the community celebration, including date, time, length, and location. Also, include this in your regular classroom newsletters and on the school website.

Make sure all the community volunteers are invited as well. Having the students who benefited from their expertise call them directly is a meaningful way for these volunteers to be included.

Have your students make posters about the community celebration and post these throughout the school.

Lastly, it is important to be positive and flexible when communicating with the school community and media about your project. Any time they can give you is valuable and better than nothing, and it will benefit you and your students.

As you can see, multiple partnerships are essential for quality service-learning projects. The more collaboration and connections you make with your community, the more meaningful the experience will be for everyone involved.

RESOURCES

School/Community Partnerships Selected Resources, at http://www.servicelearning .org/lsa/lsa_page/school_cmty.php.

Community Partners, at http://www.service-learningpartnership.org/site/PageServer?pagename=tr_communitypartners.

Chapter 6

Working in Teams

Individually we are one drop. Together, we are an ocean.

—Ryunosuke Satoro

As Dewey has taught educators, collaborative learning is a valuable way for students to make gains both academically and socially. This does not come without challenges, however, and this chapter will prepare readers for the different stages of development a group can go through during a service-learning project. Discipline suggestions will also be discussed in this section.

The skills—collaboration, teamwork, and communication—that come from working together in small groups are essential for our students. The nitty-gritty work of teams is not always easy, but in service learning (as in life) it produces the greatest rewards, products, and processes. All groups go through a learning journey together, and as educators and facilitators, we shepherd them through it, giving support, guidance, and direction as needed. Teachers embarking on service learning for the first time need to know that these teams will struggle, challenge, learn, and eventually grow to be cohesive and functioning. Many will shine and do more than they ever thought they could. Some will be dysfunctional and will need close guidance. This is all part of the process. This chapter will tell you what to expect and what to do about problems as they arise.

THE SMALL GROUP PROCESS

Much has been written about the group process and its phases. When I took my first service-learning workshop, though, my eyes popped open when I read the stages a group moves through. I had seen the struggles groups go through

Table 6.1. Tuckman's Team Development Model

Stage	Tasks	Behaviors
Forming *Polite, but little achieved*	• Establish base expectations • Identify similarities • Agree on common goals • Begin to develop trust	• Getting to know one another and bond • Dependency • Processes often ignored • Rely on leaders for structure, but not full engagement
Storming *Testing others*	• Identify power and control issues • Gain communication skills • Identify resources/ balance participation • Begin to build unity	• Express differences of ideas, feelings, and opinions • React emotionally to leadership • Independency or counterdependency • Though under pressure leader needs to be supportive, to listen, to manage conflict, and to explain decisions
Norming *Valuing differences*	• Mutual acceptance • Develop cohesion, commitment, and unity • Team norms, roles, and processes clear and accepted	• Decisions made through negotiation and consensus building • Trust and relationship building • Leader respected and acts as team member, shares leadership, helps build consensus, and enables others
Performing *Flexibility and productivity from trust*	• Achieve challenging, effective, and satisfying results • Find solutions to problems using appropriate controls • Establish autonomy and interdependency	• Collaborative work • Team members care about each other • Team establishes unique identity and behave more strategically • Leader gives projects tasks, and support; team operates on its own

Source: Jim Brenner, professor emeritus, University of California Cooperative Extension, jsbrenner@ucdavis.edu.

firsthand in the classroom and wondered, why didn't I know about these phases? So, here is a short description of each stage a group can move through. Next, I will share how this model applies to service-learning groups.

Forming

In service learning, this is the exciting beginning of the project, when students are seeing who their team is and are sharing ideas, exploring possibilities, and learning how they might function together. With elementary-, middle-, and high-school students, there is lots of enthusiastic discussion, interruption, high-volume talking, and brainstorming. Often in the forming stage, the sky is the limit. Groups want to take on the world: plant a huge garden to sustain the lunch program, build a greenhouse, create a new program, or choreograph a performance.

Students should be allowed to let their imaginations go wild for the first session, and the teacher should then guide them to discover what they might be able to accomplish in the given time. Mostly, the facilitator's role in the forming phase is to make sure all students are heard and respected, provide some reality checks, and help students shape their ideas into doable, realistic actions. All the while it will be important to protect their idealistic thinking and grand ideas. This can be a hard line to walk!

Storming

Once students are settled down into the project, likely after a week or so, the reality of what they are doing sinks in. Students begin to realize they need to work hard to achieve their lofty and agreed-upon goals. So they storm. This looks like snippiness between students, role adjusting, agitation, work, and work avoidance. During this phase students are trying to figure out what their role is exactly, and how they fit in.

Some students are used to complaining about a group or group members and then having a teacher solve the problem for them. This might be a teacher deciding on a solution, or giving students the chance to work in alternate teams or on their own. This is not a great way to handle the storming stage. Students here need to learn to persevere. They need to learn to commit and stick with their goals. What a valuable life lesson!

By solving problems with the team, the teacher validates that the team will continue, even with the present challenges. The teacher can meet with the team and openly discuss current issues and guide students to solutions, but not solve them for them. Questions such as "What can this team do to work through this?" and "How can we solve this together?" build a sense of team problem solving and camaraderie.

Students will make it through the storming stage. Most will make it through with limited guidance needed from the teacher, depending on the age and skill set of the students. Some will need more explicit adult involvement. Soon enough, they will head into the lovely norming and performing stages, and it all will be worth it!

Norming (and Sometimes Even Performing!)

Now the team is humming along with their project, each knowing what to do, and coming together to share and work toward the next goal. Students are positive, engaged, and focused. They are clear on their roles and communicate well with each other. Students are primarily independent in this phase and are building confidence and skills. They usually stay in this phase until the completion of the project. Feeling that level of cooperation and collaboration is empowering and motivating for students, and many great things can be accomplished within these beautiful phases of service learning.

GENERAL GUIDELINES

Of course, your students might not progress through these phases in this order, or they might fall back into one or another (particularly storming!). So, realize that every group is different, just as every learner is different, and their struggles are normal.

Knowing the phases is incredibly helpful because it prepares you for what to expect, generally. If you know that the group is "storming," within limits, you can let them storm and see if they can work it out. Just knowing these are a normal part of group work can take a lot of pressure off the teacher. When I first started using service learning I found the idea that groups storm to be incredibly helpful. I did not know this was a normal part of group work and the process. So, by framing the work in this way, I was better prepared and able to help my students in these phases.

HIGH-ENERGY GROUPS (WITH STUDENTS WHO HAVE SOME BEHAVIOR ISSUES)

Inevitably, you will have some high-energy groups that need some attention and guidance with focus issues. Often, the idea of student-led learning is overwhelmingly exciting for these learners. It seems so free that they have a hard time breaking down tasks into meaningful chunks and following through. This is where your role as the facilitator is essential.

For groups that are behaviorally unfocused, you will need to facilitate their timetable and to-do list. This will need to be guided, with very discrete actions that can be assigned to individuals or pairs. Preferably, the first few should be shorter-term actions as well, such as making a phone call, e-mailing an expert, or getting a question answered through research. That way, these learners find success and engagement in a positive way and learn how the project works. Usually, with guidance and smaller, broken-down tasks, these students are successful.

Occasionally, though, this will not be the case. A student (or two) might be too overwhelmed by the freedom and opportunity a project like this offers. So, clear expectations, small tasks, and the outlining of consequences are necessary. Teachers should use their regular discipline routine with these students. Logical consequences, such as working independently, for a set amount of time is a good motivator. Students want to be involved in these projects. They are exciting, social, engaging, and meaningful. Students who miss out for behavioral reasons often change their behavior so they can be involved again with their team.

In the rare case when this simply does not happen, a student can be paired with a paraprofessional or can complete a modified project independently. This is not ideal and every effort to help a student stay in a team should be made, including involvement with parents and the principal. If this is overwhelming for the teacher, and causes the other students to suffer, then this is a last option that can be utilized.

In most cases, you will find that high-energy, hard-to-focus students will thrive with service learning. At times, they simply need a little more direction and involvement. This might mean you will need more supervision in your classroom. Parent volunteers, special educators, and school support staff can provide some assistance, if you need it, with this situation.

In some cases, paraprofessionals will already be working with students on Individualized Education Plans (IEPs) or on 504 plans (plans to accommodate a student need or disability) in your classroom. These educational professionals can work with particular groups if there is a student with a behavioral or academic disability, offering to serve as mentors to particular teams of students. This support provides the necessary guidance for most students to have great success with service learning.

ONE STUDENT DOES IT ALL

This is a standard problem in all group work. We have all seen it happen. One student takes over and does most of the work in a group project. One of the main focuses of service learning is for students to develop skills of collaboration, teamwork, communication, goal setting, and organization. It benefits no one if one student is doing most of the work and does not honor the process.

Luckily, meeting with the involved team is an option that can change this problem quickly. It is essential that the educational leader reads the timeline and to-do list, making sure that the jobs are equally distributed. Students might need some guidance here, as assigning tasks is a new skill.

One key part of this problem is for all students to relinquish control of the project to each other. Sometimes, you will have a perfectionist student, one who wants to succeed and likes to be in charge. This student might need a one-on-one conversation about the nature of the service learning and how group work is essential for the success of the project. There are two common areas of assessment in a model I use for service learning: the portfolio and the project. If a portfolio assessment is used, that will be the individual score for the student. The project is graded as group (or if needed, individually). The portfolio can be a place where a committed, high-achieving student can find the control and personal success he or she is craving. They obviously can contribute greatly to the project as well, but having two different assessments, one individual and one group, can alleviate some of the self-imposed stress that high-achieving students might be feeling and give them a chance to meet and exceed standards.

High-achieving students can also take on higher-level and more challenging aspects of the project. The facilitation and guidance of the teacher is helpful here; you can guide students in teams to select doable, challenging goals for their particular level and skill set. For example, for one student, writing interview questions for a local judge, and then calling or setting up the interview might be overwhelming. But for some, this is the right level of challenge. Use what you know about your students to guide them with proper and logical assignments within their groups.

SPECIAL-EDUCATION STUDENTS

It is worth mentioning again that students of all abilities and backgrounds can be successful with service learning. The team aspect, student interest and choice, and the idea of solving community and school problems is very empowering and exciting to most students. In many cases, with the above suggestions, these students will find success within these projects.

To plan for projects with special-education students, teachers and special educators should meet prior to the beginning of the project, and throughout it as well, to monitor special-education students. Here are some things that have worked to support special-education students:

- Find alternative research materials at the student's reading level.
- Provide graphic organizers and other visuals for key concepts.
- Break apart group duties into very specific small steps. Use checklists and cross off tasks as they are accomplished.
- Guide students in positive interactions with the community, school staff, and other students.
- Encourage alternative formats. Most students are used to writing assignments, which can be difficult for students who struggle with reading and writing. They might be surprised and excited to perform a skit, sing a song, or build a model.

The group work in service learning is a dynamic, challenging, and rewarding process for students. It is not always easy. But together students can accomplish great and meaningful things. They need a teacher who can guide them through the phases and challenges while helping them maintain control and investment in the project. Using these tips can help you make this process smoother and more effective. As you gain experience using service learning with your students, you will develop your own set of group management techniques that work for your students and learning environment.

Explain that by giving students choice and voice, you are giving them power and privilege. Explain that if they abuse it, they lose it. Help your students realize you are taking a chance by doing unconventional education—you are giving them the benefit of the doubt, the trust, and the chance to make a difference. This sets the tone for a collective journey, a collective risk, a collective path that you are on together. Once the students realize this, they will ultimately work harder, dig deeper, and learn more than they ever could have imagined.

RESOURCES

Jacoby, B. (2003). *Building Partnerships for Service Learning.* San Francisco: Jossey-Bass.

Chapter 7

Authentic Assessments

The difference between school and life? In school, you're taught a lesson and then given a test. In life, you're given a test that teaches you a lesson.

—Tom Bodett

Students need to have academic accountability within these projects to meet curricular goals. During this chapter, readers will learn how to create and gather meaningful assessments for the service-learning process. Included will be an example of a portfolio assessment I have used successfully with my students. This can be modified as a powerful assessment tool for any service-learning project in any content area. There will also be lists and descriptions of multiple and varied assessment opportunities.

Many teachers love the idea of service learning but wonder where the assessment or the evidence of learning is. Assessments for service learning need to be carefully planned to reflect the learning expectations developed. Having various assessments for the project allows teachers to grade various parts of the service-learning experience, to get a full view of the learning journey.

For service learning to be academically successful, it must be firmly rooted in curricular goals and show evidence of learning that can be assessed. This can be done by utilizing several assessments in concert. (Don't worry! It is not as hard as you think!) This chapter will describe one successful model and give many ideas for others as well.

THE IMPORTANCE OF ASSESSMENT
IN SERVICE LEARNING

Numerous studies have shown that high-quality service learning enhances student learning (Eyler and Giles, 1999–2001), and in order to do so, this learning needs to be carefully monitored and assessed. According to Steinke and Fitch (2007), "Systematic assessments of service learning provide opportunities to demonstrate the powerful impact that this pedagogy can have on student learning."

Ideally, assessment should happen throughout the project. According to a Vermont Community Works guide to service-learning, assessment

- is complex and multidimensional.
- centers on feedback.
- is rooted in context (i.e., situational).
- can be done by the teacher and students.
- is both informal and formal.
- is ongoing (i.e., it should occur not just when work is done but while students are working and learning).

(National Service Learning Assessment Study Group, 1999)

THE PORTFOLIO ASSESSMENT

This is an independent portfolio that each student must complete as part of the project. It contains timelines, vocabulary, education records and activities, information, and built-in reflection about the service-learning project. One portfolio sample is shared in appendixes 7.1–7.12.

The portfolio is a key piece of assessment because it builds into the project an individual level of accountability. Students know they are each responsible for writing down the timeline, taking notes, listing new vocabulary, and more. By not falling back on one person, or one portfolio, there is an individual accountability and opportunity for each child to succeed. Each student monitors his or her own learning by using this assessment, and teachers can get a clear perspective on the progress of each student throughout the experience.

Students will need reminders and encouragement to work on their portfolios in the project. If used well, it is a guide for the project itself, and it contains a record of the individual's whole learning process, from the opening brainstorm to the final reflection.

POSSIBLE PORTFOLIO PARTS

You will find a cover sheet in appendix 7.1 for the portfolio I have been using with middle-level students for years. It includes

- a learning and brainstorming web;
- planning sheets for the project;
- a timeline (to be organized and completed by the team);
- journal entries (for built-in learning reflection);
- project notes and information, which can include vocabulary sheets, supporting questions, presentation notes, content area reading notes, research and information, diagrams, and drawings and charts; and
- self-assessments (weekly group and self-assessments).

For more information on the parts of a portfolio, see appendix 7.1. You can tailor the portfolio to require any type of learning evidence you would like to see in the project. What if the project is math related? Ask for diagrams and specific math work to support the learning and project. What if it is in Spanish? Have students include writing samples in their portfolios. The portfolio is where you can ask for specific types of learning evidence that will emerge from the project, and if it does not, then you can guide students to research or find other learning activities to gain the knowledge to provide these portfolio pieces.

AUTHENTIC ASSESSMENTS (VISUAL AND WRITTEN)

I recommend having two components for a project assessment rubric, a written and a visual. This allows for multiple ways to demonstrate learning and knowledge. Service learning has a culminating event in which students share their work. Sharing it in visual and linguistic formats is powerful. Rubrics for these are included in appendix 7.9.

Students can complete projects that have both components. Some examples of combination projects that include both written and visual requirements are

- a field guide with written species information and pictures of individual species;
- a poster presentation with written information about the topic, graphs and illustrations;
- a play performance, including the script and the actual video;

- a garden plot with a guide of plant and seed types, growth patterns, and other information;
- a letter-writing campaign with illustrations or pictures of the environmental problem;
- a draft of a bill for the legislature that includes a map of how the bill will pass through various levels of government before becoming law;
- a picture book written by upper-elementary, middle- or high- school students for younger grades with detailed text and illustrations;
- a presentation or speech with visual components;
- a PowerPoint presentation with text, images, diagrams, and illustrations;
- writing tasks (interview, letter, press release, report, song or poem, journal, picture book, field guide) shared with the school community;
- a game show (evaluate content with specific criteria); and
- a reflection journal with images.

Text Box 7.1

Characteristics of Good Tasks for Standards-Based Learning

- focus on applying important concepts and essential skills.
- align with at least one standard.
- have a real-life application.
- demand high-level thinking skills (analysis, synthesis, evaluation).
- culminate in a product that can be scored (e.g., written report, essay, letter, graph, chart, table; speech or multimedia presentation; instruction for a specific audience; a three-dimensional model).
- allow for multiple types of communication.
- require more than a simple right or wrong answer.

These are just a few ideas from different subject areas; there are countless more. What is key with each of these projects is that you are looking for linguistic and visual learning and processing.

ASSESSING CIVIC RESPONSIBILITY

One of the strongest gains in service learning is how it is linked to the development of students' civic responsibility and engagement. As stated in a previous chapter, students who participate in service learning have higher levels of community engagement; are more likely to volunteer, participate, and vote; and become productive, responsible citizens.

7.2 Civic Responsibility Rubric

Criteria	0 No Demonstration	1 Attempted Demonstration	2 Partial Demonstration	3 Proficient Demonstration	4 Sophisticated Demonstration
Personal	Unaware of responsible personal behavior	Recognizes responsible personal behavior but is unable to explain its importance in a physical activity setting	Able to explain responsible personal behavior but is unable to demonstrate it consistently in a physical activity setting	Able to explain and demonstrate responsible personal behavior in a physical activity setting, including safe and appropriate etiquette and conduct	Able to explain the importance and impact of responsible personal behavior in society
Social	Unable to recognize a competent leader and/or group mentor	Recognizes a competent leader and/or group member, but is unable to identify the skills necessary to function as one	Able to identify the leadership and membership skills necessary to function as a member of a team in a school, family, or community setting and the causes of conflict within these settings	Able to describe and demonstrate the leadership and membership skills necessary to function as a member of a team in a school, family, or community setting and to use strategies to prevent or solve conflict within these settings	Consistently acts as a leader and as a productive group member in a variety of school, family, and/or community settings and incorporates conflict prevention or resolution skills into daily experiences
Civic	Unable to identify a public policy issue in our democracy	Able to identify a public policy issue in our democracy	Able to identify and describe a public policy issue in our democracy	Able to identify and evaluate a public policy issue in our democracy and to explain the importance of active, informed attentive citizen participation in addressing that issue	Actively participates in solving a civic problem and articulates the impact of his/her actions on public policy and constitutional democracy

Adapted by Katy Farber and used with permission of Community Works Institute, www.communityworks institute.org.

This type of education is hard to measure, but a few rubrics have been developed to focus on this area. Here is one from Community Works Institute. I consider a score of 3 as meeting the standard, and a 4 as exceeding the standards.

ASSESSING ORAL PRESENTATIONS

During a service-learning sharing time—be it a parent night, all school celebration, or classroom festival—students will have the opportunity to present their work orally. This is another chance for assessment. Many teachers know students who cannot demonstrate their learning in writing, but they can showcase it beautifully orally. By adding this to your arsenal of assessments, you will have more information about your students' learning, particularly with students who might not demonstrate it otherwise.

There are many great oral presentation rubrics out there. You might have one that works for your students. If not, part of the service-learning project assessment in appendix 7.9 is the presentation criteria. You could use this, another presentation rubric, or add a presentation component or your overall project rubric. Learning to present orally with good presentation skills is a lifelong skill to master, and students can develop these as well as their content knowledge within service-learning projects.

ASSESSING TEAMWORK

One key element of service learning is how students use their teamwork skills of cooperation, communication, respect, and commitment. Students will be challenged and grow in numerous ways in this area during their projects. They will need to know that teamwork is part of their assessment and grade, and that teams need to work together to succeed. Of course, there will always be challenges in this area, but the key is how students work through it. Utilizing a teamwork rubric to judge this progress and learning is essential. The teacher, volunteers, and students can give feedback about how a team is working (or not working!) together. I have included a teamwork rubric in appendix 7.11, and hopefully it works for your class. If not, I have listed more resources at the end of this chapter.

INVOLVE STUDENTS IN SELF-ASSESSMENT

When you have decided on your assessment plan, and before you launch fully into the project, it is a good idea to go through your assessments (checklists, rubrics, or others) in detail with your class. This way students will have a clear idea of what is expected of them. It is even better to have examples of grade level work to share with your students.

As part of your students' experience with service learning, self-assessment can promote self-analysis, a deeper exploration of learning goals, and a clearer picture of the student's perceptions and learning process.

Explain to students that they will be assessing their own work just as you will be. They will use the same rubrics to grade their work and submit this with their projects. This is particularly helpful with the teamwork rubrics, where students often have strong opinions and insight into the interworking of a group.

When used in this way, self-assessment can be a learning tool and provide more insight for the teacher. In every assessment you use with service learning, I encourage you to have students self-assess their work.

TEACH THE RUBRICS, AND USE EXAMPLES

For students to understand the assessments, a few class periods need to be focused on walking through the materials, using examples, modeling behaviors, and allowing for discussion and questions. Read through everything with your students and allow ample time to explain and show examples. Sending copies home to the parents is also a great way to keep them informed about the project and enlist some volunteer assistance.

Text Box 7.2

Assessment Idea Overview

1. *Teacher observation* could be used to determine how well students master the skills needed for the project.
2. A *rubric* is an excellent way to evaluate student products. Delineating criteria for numerical scales can help clarify expectations for students.
3. Students could use a *checklist* to self-assess their progress in planning the cleanup.
4. A *journal* or *learning log* could be used as a self-assessment tool. Journals also provide a way for students to reflect upon their learning and development cognitive skills.
5. Students could produce a variety of evidence that demonstrates their knowledge and skills. In addition to graphs, students might explain in writing why they chose a particular type of graph. Students might also discuss problems they confronted in their work on this project and how they addressed these. Gathering a wider variety of evidence allows for a more valid and reliable picture of student learning.

Source: The National Service-Learning and Assessment Study Group, 1999.

Rubrics can be tricky when different numbers signify different levels of student achievement. For some rubrics, 3 is meeting the standard; for others it is 4 or even 5. The numbers are variable. It is helpful to use one number system throughout the project, so students and parents do not get confused Make sure it is clear to students and parents what each number means in a rubric assessment (better yet—label it right on the rubric).

Through the years I have kept examples of projects to share with future classes. This is not possible for those just starting out, but you can start to digitally record the projects so you do not have to collect large projects over the years (save classroom space!). You can do this with digital photography, flip videos, or on class websites.

The Responsive Classroom model of classroom management works very well as a whole class or as a whole school program. It also ties in very nicely with service learning. Responsive Classroom

is an approach to elementary teaching that emphasizes social, emotional, and academic growth in a strong and safe school community. The goal is to enable optimal student learning. Created by classroom teachers and backed by evidence from independent research, the Responsive Classroom approach is based on the premise that children learn best when they have both academic and social-emotional skills. The approach therefore consists of classroom and school wide practices for deliberately helping children build academic and social-emotional competencies. (Responsive Classroom, 2010)

This type of organizational structure in a classroom provides students with a social framework to engage in the work of service learning.

The process of developing a strong class community will only help facilitate more powerful and enriching service-learning projects with your students.

Teachers have known that service learning—that is, students solving community problems—is a motivating and rich tool for learning. What has been more difficult is for teachers to quantify this learning. By establishing learning goals and developing tools to assess them, teachers can not only justify the merit and worth of service-learning projects but guide students to more specific and clear learning outcomes. By using the tools and ideas in this chapter, I hope you have a better sense of how you can plan service-learning assessments more easily.

RESOURCES

Service Learning and Assessment: A Field Guide for Teachers, at http://www.communityworks.org/cwpublications/slassessguide/slassessguide.html.
Assessment, Evaluation and Performance Measurement: Selected Resources, at http://www.servicelearning.org/instant_info/bibs/he_bibs/assess_eval.

Chapter 8

Powerful Reflection

A mind that is stretched by a new experience can never go back to its old dimensions.

—Oliver Wendell Holmes

Reflection is an integral part of service learning. As in education, with our fast-paced, increasing expectations, and sense of urgency, it is something that is often overlooked. For students engrossed in service learning, reflection opportunities provide a chance to think about this new on-the-ground, real-life learning. And the results are powerful. It just takes time and encouragement from the teacher.

Luckily, there are many ways to provide reflection to your students during the unit, and they do not have to take much time from the project itself. Each teacher should find what works for them. Consider frequency, format, and duration. Below are some of the ideas I have seen that work well.

BEST PRACTICES FOR DESIGNING REFLECTION

When creating reflection opportunities in your service-learning projects, it is helpful to keep the guidelines below, from the Service Learning website (servicelearning.org), in mind.

Reflection activities work best when they are designed well, planned in advance, and implemented thoughtfully. Reflection is a continuous process and activities can occur at any time during the process. Effective reflection incorporates the following best practices:

1. Reflection should occur before the service-learning experience, during the experience, and after the experience.
2. Reflection activities should clearly link the service-learning experience to academic standards and curriculum objectives.
3. Frequent opportunities for discussion of service should be provided so students can interact with their peers, mentors, and those they serve.
4. Reflection activities should challenge students to test assumptions about their values and to explore, clarify, and alter their values.
5. Students should be included in the planning of reflection activities so that they have ownership of the process.
6. Reflection activities should incorporate various learning styles (visual, auditory, kinesthetic) and experiences to encourage students to think in different ways.
7. Teachers should provide continual feedback to students so they can improve their critical thinking and analytical skills during the reflective process.
(Bringle and Hatcher, 1999; Conrad and Hedin, 1997; Eyler and Giles, 1999; Eyler, Giles, and Schmiede, 1996; Toole and Toole, 1995).
(*Source:* http://www.servicelearning.org/instant_info/fact_sheets/k-12_facts/reflection)

OPPORTUNITIES FOR REFLECTION

During service learning, you can provide frequent, informal reflection opportunities for your students rather easily. It is helpful during these times to take notes on the students' discussion and reflections so you can provide feedback so students can improve. I recommend using all of the ideas listed below during your service-learning projects with students. Here are a few ways to provide these short but meaningful opportunities for reflection:

• Small group check-ins: When students are engaged in small-group project work, the teachers, support staff, and even parent volunteers can visit with groups and check in on their progress. Ask students to reflect on what is working, what they need help with, and new knowledge gained during their particular project. This will provide small snippets of reflection (see small-group reflection question ideas in appendix 8.1).
• Whole-class big questions: At the end of class, it is a good idea to gather the whole class to share reflections. This way, students can learn from each other it is normal to face challenges, and share any interesting or inspiring knowledge gained from working on their projects. This also allows for groups to cross-collaborate. One group, for example, might be working on developing a wildflower garden and another on butterfly habitats. These teams can work together and share information if they are aware of the

work the other group is doing. A list of general whole-class reflection questions is listed in appendix 8.2.

- One-on-one discussions: These are a great way to see how an individual student is developing in the service-learning process. It is particularly helpful to check in with both low- and high-achieving students to gauge their involvement, needs, and participation in the project. Students are sometimes more receptive to speaking about challenges in a one-on-one setting. As much as possible, document these discussions. It will help you with your all-around assessment, to troubleshoot, and to monitor the learning and reflection happenings with students. I like to have one notebook that I carry around to document these one-on-one conversations; also, I have support staff either give me feedback that I write down in this notebook, or they write it down and I attach it within. This is also a great place to record your reflections about the project as the project unfolds.
- Student journals: There are many ways to use journals for service-learning reflection. It can be a powerful reflection tool. I suggest a balance of the different types of journal entries below. These can be included in a portfolio assessment (as described in chapter 7) or as a stand-alone assessment and reflection.
  - Students can free write or respond to a list of prompts.
  - Students focus on new learning: one thing you learned, a diagram to support it, and a connection you made. One due every week.
  - Assign specific journal assignments for older students (thought-provoking, critical-thinking questions).
- Sketchbooks: These can be used in conjunction with verbal and written reflection to provide opportunities for students to use their multiple intelligences. Students may need to draw designs for projects, diagrams from their research, or images that reflect their new learning and teamwork process.
- Question or big-idea list: Often during these projects, students think of many more questions. And they often come to big ideas and conclusions in their work. These can be recorded on a paper and reflected upon in a small or large group. In a portfolio used for assessment, reflections can be embedded. Weekly team reflections can show problem areas as well as the personal development of a student (see appendix 8.2). Unit reflections also give a window into the thinking of students at the end of a service-learning experience. This can be invaluable as the teacher reflects and plans for the next service-learning project, and to help communicate to parents how the student was feeling about his or her work.

Text Box 8.1

More Ideas for Student Reflection

Classroom Journal: In this exercise, students reflect upon their class-mates' and teacher's journal entries. Prompt your students by writing the first entry. Then, each day, have a different student take the journal home and write an entry that reflects upon the most recent contribution before their own.

Community Journal: A community journal is one that the students share with the community agency staff or community members during a service-learning project. At the agency or work site, students ask community members to add an entry to the journal about their project experience or work at the agency. To get the ball rolling, you should prompt the community members with journaling ideas. Try to collect as many community entries as there are students in your class. After the service-learning project is over, assign students different community entries upon which to reflect and respond.

Classroom Discussions: These can be one of the most stimulating forms of reflection for service learning. Discussing real-world issues and themes that are relevant to the service-learning project provides students with an opportunity to explore critical thinking skills, communication skills, and current events with their peers.

Here are a few suggestions for making your classroom discussions more exciting and productive:

1. Invite a community representative to lead the discussion.
2. Have each student take a turn at leading the discussion.
3. Cut out articles from the newspaper that relate to the service-learning project and have the students discuss the broader issues that are involved.
4. Videotape each discussion and make a reflective video at the end of the project, so that students remember the issues discussed and the results of each discussion.
5. Have each student bring an object related to the service-learning project (tool, photograph, etc.) to the discussion and share the relevance of the object to their service-learning experience.

Visual Arts: Another way to introduce reflection into your classroom in a more creative way. Paint and paper or digital media can be very compelling mediums for both younger and older students to express their thoughts about their service-learning experiences. Any of these ideas can help get you started:

Photographic Journal: Instead of having students simply write in journals, have them take photographs of the service-learning project and write journal entries in response to the photographs they have taken.

Project Website: Many students have a real knack for website design. As your project progresses, have the students create a website so that their service-learning project can be shared in cyberspace with parents, students, community members, and project partners.

Bulletin Boards: School bulletin boards that are in public areas of the school can be a great way for students to share their service-learning project with the student body, teachers, and school administration. Have your class adopt one of the school's bulletin boards and keep everyone updated about what is going on with service-learning. Students can take pictures of the project and post them, as well as post other literature related to the project, such as thank-you letters from community members written in response to the project.

Source: Adapted from PSLA, 2002.

There are many resources available to educators about leading reflections with your students throughout the service-learning process. It can be overwhelming. Below I picked a few resources in case you need more ideas and resources than this book offers.

By providing both informal and quick-reflection opportunities, and more formal, culminating reflections, you will provide your students with deeper learning experiences and have more of an effect on their lives. Reflection makes service learning richer for students and provides valuable feedback for teachers. This, in turn, can help teachers reflect on the service-learning process and improve their practice.

RESOURCES

Partial article about the importance of reflection in service learning, at http://www. questia.com/googleScholar.qst;jsessionid=LN2F2Gxh2NLRpRXm8Z3knbpYh GkgXbnfKhnq0gwHb1vpS4sk1PQ3!-363574528!1384420092?docId=500054 0302.

Middle- and high-school reflection ideas, at http://www.indianacampuscompact.org/
   LinkClick.aspx?fileticket=ppeN2QOZDHo%3D&tabid=174&mid=826.
More reflection ideas at http://www.paservicelearning.org/Project_Ideas/Reflection.
   html.
"Facilitating Reflection: A Manual for Educators," at http://www.uvm.edu/~dewey/
   reflection_manual.
"Connecting Thinking and Action: Ideas for Service-Learning Reflection" (great
   reflection ideas and activities grades pre-K–12), at http://www.servicelearning.org/
   filemanager/download/132/Reflection%20Guide%20Internet1.pdf.
"The Reflection Toolkit" (it offers the benefits of reflection and activities grouped
   by time needed), at http://nationalserviceresources.org/files/legacy/filemanager/
   download/615/nwtoolkit.pdf.
Reflection in K–12 service learning at http://www.servicelearning.org/instant_info/
   fact_sheets/K-12_facts/reflection.

Chapter 9

Securing Funding

We refuse to believe that there is insufficient funds in the great vaults of opportunity of this nation.

—Dr. Martin Luther King Jr.

If I hear "in these difficult economic times" or "these tough economic times" again, I think I might be sick. Yes, I know we are in the worst recession since the Great Depression, and everyone is suffering. And schools are taking a direct hit. Programs cut, budgets slashed, and teachers being laid off. None of this is easy or in the best interest of students.

But it is our reality, harsh as it may be. So educators who want to do this revolutionary work have to think creatively to make it happen. The good thing is, it does not have to cost much. And with some planning, teachers can cover any expenses during projects pretty easily.

What sort of costs come up? Small groups might want to plant a garden, make signs, perform a play, or create a book, to list only a few examples. These activities usually take some specific materials to make them happen fully. This chapter will help you figure out how to get these materials at a minimal cost.

SCHOOL-BASED FUNDING

School-based funding is by far the best way to ensure consistent funding for service-learning projects. At budgeting time, teachers build materials and supplies into their classroom budgets, just as a teacher would for pencils, books, paper, and other supplies.

Many principals are excited and motivated about service learning and will support adding funds for these materials in their budgets. This takes meeting with your principal during budgeting time and advocating for these funds. How much? That depends on how many students, the duration of the project, and its scope, of course. But estimating about $350 for about 25 students is a good place to start.

Some principals are reluctant to support budgeting changes or increases. Showing them the many ways service learning improves academic success and civic engagement, decreases the dropout rate, and increases school attendance (see chapter 2), can convince them. You might need to do a presentation for the school board about service learning. (Don't slam this book shut! It's not that bad!) You can use the data from this book, and the resources listed at the end of the book (and each chapter) to help you. They will likely be convinced of service learning's greatness and fund your work fully.

If not, don't fear; there are other options.

RAISE THE RESOURCES

This is not as daunting as it sounds. There are several options to help you raise money or find materials for your service-learning projects.

Parent Donations

In your class newsletters and on your website, you could simply write about your planned project and ask for donations. This way, parents with fewer economic resources will not feel as if they have to contribute, but those who are comfortable and willing might donate just what you need. You know your community, their economic levels, and how they might react to this, so this may be a tool you use or ultimately skip altogether.

Homegrown Fund-Raisers

You know what I am talking about—bake sales, car washes, and the like. You can organize and run one of these. If you find your projects in need of materials, getting them could be as easy as requesting students to bake something and bring it to the next basketball game for a bake sale. Of course, if the project is huge, you will have to coordinate a much larger effort.

Homegrown fund-raisers that link to projects are terrific too, such as building birdhouses to sell to support an environmental set of projects. Parents are usually willing to help out, materials can be donated, and everyone can meet on a Saturday to create something of value, such as birdhouses, pasta sauce, bat boxes, or any other creative ideas.

These fund-raisers are wonderful because they are linked to communities and their needs. You can utilize your community contacts and resource people to help generate ideas for small fund-raisers to support your projects.

Environmental Fund-Raisers for Schools

Many great programs have popped up in the last several years to help schools with fund-raising. It is much easier for busy teachers and small groups to raise funds than ever before.

I am not going to advocate for any magazine or candy sales, as they do not seem in line with the goals of service learning, healthy living, and local communities. There are green and sustainable fund-raising organizations that are worth looking into if you are undertaking a very large project and would like to have full funding in place before you begin.

Environmental fund-raising groups: These organizations help schools by supplying environmentally friendly projects such as fair-trade coffee and chocolate, no-waste lunch kits, and reusable water bottles. Schools take a significant portion of the profits, and they are promoting greener lifestyles in the process.

Eco-Label Fundraising: http://ecolabelfundraising.com.

Green Raising: http://www.greenraising.com.

Mother Earth Fundraising: http://www.motherearthfundraising.com.

Green Students Fundraising: http://www.greenstudentsfundraising.com.

Green 4 My School: http://www.green4myschool.com.

Environmental T-shirt sales: There are several companies that sell environmental T-shirts that also give a portion of their profits to schools. These are great T-shirts that everyone likes—they share educational messages, and they support schools. These T-shirts can be found at http://www.jimmorrist-shirts.com/fundrinfo.htm and http://www.ecosprouts.com.

Local Businesses and Banks

Many local businesses and banks are happy to support schools, especially if they can gain some good marketing out of it. In one service-learning project in which students created a community magazine, the students sold local businesses advertising space to fund the project. It might just take a visit from a few students to motivate local businesses to contribute to a school community project.

Local Rotary or Kiwanis Clubs

These clubs often participate in charitable donations to the community. Often they have community donations written into their budgets and want to support meaningful work. A well-written letter to a club about the project might yield significant funding and community involvement.

COMMUNITY-BASED GRANTS

Take a look at your local non-profits. What ones exist to support schools? To support the local environment or civic engagement? Likely there is an organization supporting the type of work you intend to do. All it might take is a call explaining your project and what type of support you need.

Ask your principal and superintendent if they are aware of any local groups, then try the community pages of your phone book for contacts. I know you are a teacher, and this is not something you want to spend your time doing. Truthfully, you might not even need to with the other funding options—but if you need to, you can. Someone on your school staff is likely to know about a group that might support your work as well, so mention it at a staff meeting (or in an e-mail).

For a few years, a local non-profit would supply my class with just enough funds necessary to get the materials for student groups. I would often be in the middle of my work on projects with students and discover a financial need. I would inquire, explain what it was for, and I was granted the funds every time.

There are larger, more corporate grants available as well. Here is a list of those, but this is only a preliminary search—there are countless more. It is a starting point if you need to look into this type of funding.

Funding sources list:

National Service Learning Partnership: http://www.service-learningpartnership. org/site/PageServer?pagename=tr_funding.
Servicelearning.org: http://www.servicelearning.org/funding-sources.
Wisconsin Department of Public Instruction: http://dpi.wi.gov/fscp/slupdate. html.

Grant and funding opportunities:

Project Learning Tree: http://www.plt.org/cms/pages/21_22_18.html.
Youth Service America: http://www.ysa.org/grants.
Toyota Tapestry Grants: http://www.nsta.org/pd/tapestry.

MAKE DO WITH WHAT YOU HAVE

Here is a little secret—aside from the support my class received for my first few years in service learning, I have not received any outside funds other than from parents or from within the school. And in our current economic reality (oh no, I said it myself!), most teachers will find themselves in this boat. We are forever resourceful, as teachers, and often must simply make do with what we have (or don't have).

Schools have loads of stuff. Stuff in storage, closets, out of sight, or piled high. In many cases, it is a matter of finding what you need. So I often send e-mails to the staff requesting this or that, and most materials have appeared in a matter of days. The custodian is also one to maintain a strong appreciation for and relationship with. He or she can point you to tons of gear you might need for your students' work. For us, it was shovels, a wheelbarrow, and some soil, signposts, wood, and paint. This type of reuse is environmentally responsible as well!

Parents and volunteers are often able to lend materials, or buy a few for groups. And the longer you do this, the more materials your classroom will have to be ready for the next year (just be ready to ask for that storage shed out back).

If you have older students, funding can be part of their projects and their jobs. High-school students can realize what they need and develop a way to get it. How compelling it is when articulate and dedicated high-school students request funding from the principal! Any way you can release responsibility back to the students will make it a richer experience with more buy-in and ownership from the students.

So don't let your budget woes, or a lack of funding, stop you from service learning. In most cases, you can do it without much financial support. If you find yourself needing some funds for your students, don't fear; just try one of the ideas listed above and you will likely get what you need.

List of ideas for doing with what you have:

- Contact your custodian.
- Contact your school staff.
- Contact your school administration.
- Contact parents.
- Contact community members.
- Lurk in storage areas for what you need.
- Look on Freecycle.com for what you need.
- Look on Craiglist.com for what you need.

- Contact your local solid waste company and tell them what your needs are in case someone has recently thrown out usable supplies (hardware, wood, nails, etc.).

There are many resources out there to support your great work in service learning. Start with your own school and community, then reach out if you find a need with your service-learning projects. People love to support real and meaningful work with children in their own communities.

Chapter 10

Voices from the Field

Inspiration, Advice, and Guidance from Teachers Currently Leading Service-Learning Projects

Listen and learn from people who have already been where you want to go. Benefit from their mistakes instead of repeating them.

—Benjamin Carson

There are so many teachers across this country doing amazing work in the area of service learning. From them you can find inspiration, words of wisdom, and practical advice. I have interviewed four teachers from different regions of the United States teaching different subject areas to give you a sense of what some teachers are doing with their students. This is only a beginning—I am sure there are thousands of teachers across the country doing this type of work.

Take what you can from them. Teachers need to share with each other, listen to each other, and inspire each other in this important work.

Here is an interview from a seventh-grade social studies teacher, Marlo Dentice, with additional support from Sarah Bush. You will see how he integrated service learning with his social studies curriculum and provided for reflection; and the project did not require much funding.

SCHOOL: GREENDALE MIDDLE SCHOOL

1. *Provide a brief description/narrative of your project (include purpose/ goals, a brief timeline, and the "story").*

   A few seventh graders had asked me if our class could participate in the We the People program. We the People . . . Project Citizen introduces students to and educates them in the methods and procedures used in our political process.

69

The goal of the program is to develop students' commitment to active citizenship and governance by providing the knowledge and skills required for effective participation, providing practical experience designed to foster a sense of competence and efficacy and developing an understanding of the importance of citizen participation. This program helps the students' knowledge, enhances their skills and deepens their understanding of how "the people"—all of us—can work together to make communities better. This project started in September and it ended in May where the students presented their project at the capital (Madison).

2. *What opportunities were available for youth leadership and voice?*

This project was completely the students' idea. A few students had approached me about participating in this program. The program is completely student centered, student directed. I explained the project to them and gave them a timeline, but they decided how much they wanted to participate. I was just the supervisor that helped guide the students and made sure they were on the right track. I helped mediate the conversations and voting but the students are the ones that researched, wrote letters, and made phone calls. They challenged themselves each and every day making this project the great success it was.

3. *What "community" need did this project address?*

In the program, the students decided as a class what problem they would like to address in their community. The students really focused on the development of a public policy to deal with a specific problem in the community and the recommendation of that policy to the appropriate government or governmental agency.

As a class, the students voted on working on cleaning up the wooded area between Canterbury Elementary School and Greendale Middle School. The students decided they would try to clean up the area in the woods so that students would stop drinking and smoking or even doing drugs in the woods. The students thought by getting the police involved and constructing disc-golf in the woods there would be more people in the woods, hopefully scaring off drug users and the woods would become a safe area where students could play disc-golf and walk to school without being scared.

4. *How was your project linked to the curriculum and how did it further the academic achievement of students?*

The students study politics and government in their seventh-grade social studies class. This project helps students see how everything they are learning is really applied in real life. This project helped to make real-life connections for the students. It worked out great, we talked about something in social studies class about how everyone has a voice and then the students had the opportunity to go out into their community and apply everything they had learned to a real-life situation.

5. *How did participants have the opportunity for reflection?*

   The students had the opportunity to take a fieldtrip to the State Bar of Wisconsin, in Madison, Wisconsin. In Madison, the students presented their portfolios in a simulated legislative hearing, demonstrating their knowledge and understanding of how public policy is formulated. They presented in front of many different congressional men and women and even the State Superintendent of Public Instruction. Each student received a certificate for participating and as a class; we received a ribbon and a plaque for coming in fifth place in the state. After the trip, as a class, we discussed the project and it seemed to be an amazing experience for all the students who were involved.

6. *What were the materials, money, and "connections" needed to complete this project?*

   This project was done completely in the classroom, outside the school (walking-distance woods) and the computer lab. The only money that was needed was money for our poster board and mailing the poster board to Madison. The students wrote for grants to help finance the construction of the disc-golf.

7. *Upon reflection, what are some revisions you would make should you attempt this project again?*

   When I do this project again, I would like to try to have all four of my classes involved. This year I piloted the program and only had one class participate. I am definitely recommending this project for other classrooms to try.

8. *What were your key project successes?*

   The entire project was a success. The students were able to work together to identify a problem in the community; they studied a public policy and developed an action plan for implementing their policy. The students put all of their information together on a poster board and put together a three-ring binder with all their information. They then presented in Madison where the students did a great job of presenting their information to the congressional men and women. Greendale Middle School received fifth place in the entire state for their hard work and accomplishments. The students were very proud of their hard work and efforts. They did a great job working together as a class (teamwork). They showed tremendous amounts of maturity and growth throughout this entire project.

9. *What were your key project challenges?*

A challenge that we found while working on this project was trying to find money to pay for our disc-golf course. The students researched many companies and found out that it would cost about $15,000 to construct a disc-golf course in the woods behind the school. The students then wrote for three different grants to try to help finance this project. At this time, we have not found out about the status of those grants. This challenge did not once discourage the students because they knew they did this entire project on their own. They learned that they have a voice even though they are children and they can do anything when they put their minds together and work together.

10. *What lessons have you learned about trying to implement service learning in your classroom?*

I learned that service learning is an amazing way to help student's make connections between school curriculum and academic studies and real-life experiences. I also learned that service learning is a way to show our students that they have a voice and they can make things happen in their community even though they are students. This service-learning project started from a few students wanting to try something new and blossomed into an amazing learning experience for 29 seventh graders at Greendale Middle School. (Retrieved April 24, 2010, from http://bostonteachnet.org/greenfield/sigproj.htm)

Next is an interview with Mary Whalen, a recent recipient of a 2010 Rowland Foundation fellowship, who teaches high-school social studies at Twinfield Union School in Plainfield, Vermont.

1. *Please tell me about your project (grade level, content area, time period, events).*

I have been teaching service-learning thick-and-thin models for approximately 15 years. I have always embedded service learning into civic engagement content. I spent two years developing an action research project model and support for students across the state through the Governor's Institute on Education.

2. *Why did you start doing service learning with your students?*

Initially I began because it was an application of some of the ideas that I was teaching—such as sustainability—however I discovered that I needed students to take control of the entire process and focus on the process instead of the outcome. If I was force-feeding the project and outcome then it was my value system they were acting on and not theirs.

3. *How do you incorporate learning goals and curriculum into your service-learning projects?*

   The action research course is embedded into our social studies curriculum. I think there are very few schools that provide this opportunity for students as a credit-bearing core curriculum class. Learning goals are tied to critical-thinking skills, and civic engagement, etc.

4. *What do you find most satisfying about doing service learning? What do you find most challenging?*

   I find most satisfying that the student work has meaning to them, addresses an injustice and provides voice. Most challenging is . . . personally, teaching one course in this way is a full time class. . . . So I feel like it could always be even deeper. I've also spent two years raising lots of money to fulfill one of the action plans so the pursuing-grants activity has been huge for me.

5. *What advice would you give to someone just starting out with service learning? What do you wish you knew when you started out?*

   I think my greatest successes could not have been possible if I did not have school administration support. I was given the freedom to think out of the box and ask my own questions. I do wish I had time to reflect more, and the reflection that I have done is responsible for my being at a place where I am asking new and more difficult and more pertinent questions.

   For me, reflection and finding your own voice and being free to adjust when necessary is crucial. Service learning is a good match for me, in the way that I do it. I think teachers need to find their own way and their own style to make it personally sustaining.

6. *What do you think teachers need most to be successful doing service learning with their students?*

   I think they have to love it and do it because it is how they function and see the hope and beauty in the world. A teacher once asked our faculty when I taught at Harwood, "Do you teach for a world that is or a world that you would like to see?" I always thought I taught for a world that I would like to see, but the action research work I am doing is truly engaging me in a world that is, and it is . . . good.

   I don't think I would be as practical and invested in my kids and teaching if I thought the best that we could be was out of reach. Service learning makes me invested in what is.

Here is an interview with Virginia Hamilton, teacher of fifth- and sixth-grade gifted students in Florida. She takes an unconventional approach with her teaching by using service learning to have students assist a local animal shelter.

1. *Please tell me about your project (grade level, content area, time period, events).*

   Grades 5 and 6, gifted and academically talented students.

   Content areas are Language Arts, Math, Civic Studies, Music, Art, Computers. 2002 to present.

   Nine bus trips per month to South Animal Care Center in Melbourne and Central Brevard Humane Society in Cocoa, Florida.

2. *Why did you start doing service learning with your students?*

   I first started Canine Commandos when service learning was a requirement for gifted students. I knew that if the project was going to be a continuation year after year and be a success, I needed to find something that would interest the students. I was watching Animal Planet channel when an obedience trainer said that dogs are overlooked for adoption due to lack of training. He said that these dogs could be trained minutes a day. What goes better together than peanut butter and jelly? Dogs and kids! It was a no-brainer. So with the support of administration, county and parents, Canine Commandos was born. Everything Commando related has been student created.

3. *How do you incorporate learning goals and curriculum into your service-learning projects?*

   I use Florida's Gifted Frameworks and Sunshine State Standards. I also applied for the Gifted Curriculum Challenge Grant and was awarded $10,000. This allowed a total of 11 schools to train. All schools work on different assignments to incorporate learning. Some projects include scrapbooking, school newspapers, bulletin board updates, Claymation video, Photo Stories and writing a theme song.

4. *What do you find most satisfying about doing service learning? What do you find most challenging?*

   I am such an animal activist including being a vegetarian. Animals give so much to human life; I cannot imagine not having pets in the house. The most satisfying part is knowing these kids are making a difference; helping find homes for the dogs. The most challenging is working with a dog that does not want to cooperate AND trying to find enough time in each day for the students to work on their projects (these students are a weekly pullout, one day per month).

5. *What advice would you give to someone just starting out with service learning? What do you wish you knew when you started out?*

The advice I would give would be to find something that you are passionate about. We all do food drives and it is necessary, but is it memorable? Find a project that is sustainable. Each year we add on a new project. Next year, we'd like to contact a university with film studies to do a documentary with us. What I wish I knew when we first started is what service learning really meant. It took a few years to get the hang of it and truly understand the difference between service learning and community service.

6. *What do you think teachers need most to be successful doing service learning with their students?*

Support! I receive several contacts from organizations and one of their concerns is lack of support by their school and/or district.

Jean Berthiume was Vermont's Teacher of the Year in 2009. He has developed many service-learning projects using various models with his high-school students.

1. *Please tell me about your teaching experience, content area, grade level and the types of projects you are doing.*

I've been teaching for 15 years and started off in alternative education for the first two and for the last 13 years I've been in the social studies/ history department at Harwood Union High School. I've taught most courses offered in the department and have settled on teaching a unique and progressive civics course entitled Creating Sustainable Communities, U.S. History, a few electives such as psychology and current events. Grade level that I'm teaching now and have been for the last 5 years has been 10–12.

As for the types of projects I've done . . . I've done a wide variety of service-learning projects. To name a few:

1. Vermont Stories of Modern America: U.S. History students studying modern American History spend time researching and learning the general narrative of events such as World War II, the Korean War, Vietnam, The Red Scare and McCarthy, the Space Race, Civil Rights Movement, etc. The service project came from student inquiry regarding the effect of these events that shaped our nation on Vermont. So the class decided to collect oral history, gather evidence and artifacts from historical societies, etc. to tell a new narrative of Modern American History that was told through the portal of Vermont. Students found and

collected riveting oral histories, artifacts, and photos that enabled them to create a video that was entitled Vermont Stories of Modern America. Students made every decision about the video. Students collectively were consulted to edit the video, collected photos and short video clips to help tell the stories that they had collected, to deciding the music that best defined the era. In addition, the cover of the DVD was designed by students. Students even organized a premier for the film that celebrated the interviewees that shared their stories. A copy of the video was distributed to local historical societies, the Vermont Historical Society, and the Library of Congress.

2. Kaleidoscope Project: The Kaleidoscope Project came out of my civics class entitled Creating Sustainable Communities. In a Discrimination Unit I was teaching, students were learning about power and privilege within society. Students spend time researching discrimination stories from the Holocaust to the story of Matthew Shepard (via the Laramie Project). We then all (including myself) wrote our own discrimination stories. Before sharing these stories we discussed how we can safely share these stories with each other as a class. Students gave voice to what they need from their peers and the teacher before sharing these stories.

After spending three days or so on a list of agreements we all signed the sheet of paper that listed them. Students for the next week or so shared their stories and allowed for discussions to occur after each story. In the end a few students raised a comment/question for me and the class. The comment was, "Mr. B we get it now and understand how power and privilege is gained and acquired. How can we share with others the lessons and stories we just heard?" At that point I facilitated a discussion with the class about whether or not we could engage in a service-learning project that would make a difference within our community. Students discussed many different ideas about how they could share what they have learned and in doing so how they would further their own understanding about the problem facing our society.

A few students came back the next day and suggested why can't we take some of our stories and work with graphic design students here at Harwood and share our stories? Another student spoke up and said, "Yeah . . . teachers are always buying posters that depict adolescents somewhere else, but what would happen if we used our own faces and stories?" So at that point the Kaleidoscope Project was born. Four stories were selected from the class and appropriate measures were taken to protect and safeguard the well-being of the students whose stories were to be put on display in the halls of our school. Students surveyed the students before and a month after to see what effect these posters had on the school. Students were surprised to see that the posters positively changed the climate of our school. Other data was collected such as discipline referrals and there was a significant decrease in harassment or infractions relating to discrimination.

2. *Why did you start doing service learning with your students?*

I guess I've always done it . . . even before I even knew it was service learning.

These millennials are interested in social justice and being creative. I feel like when the audience is not just me for students that the quality of their work increases.

3. *How do you incorporate learning goals and curriculum into your service-learning projects?*

I use a couple of tools one is UbD (Understanding by Design) and secondly, the KIDS Consortium's KIDS Framework for high-quality service learning.

4. *What do you find most satisfying about doing service learning? What do you find most challenging?*

What I find most satisfying about doing service-learning is the opportunity to make learning relevant, real, and rigorous for my students. Students learn best when they can discover themselves in what they are learning.

What is most challenging . . . is that service-learning is not always a linear path!

5. *What advice would you give to someone just starting out with service learning? What do you wish you knew when you started out?*

My advice to someone just starting out . . . start small and help your students connect what they are learning to the world around them. Allow your students to discover authentic needs with your school or greater community. Give students an opportunity to make sense of a situation, need within the community, or how to see a problem from multiple perspectives.

6. *What do you think teachers need most to successfully do service learning with their students?*

Teachers need to have good facilitation skills and a good understanding of ethnography so that teachers don't fall into the trap of simply doing community service.

These are just a few examples of teachers who are currently using service learning in their classrooms with great success. Take the little gems from them: resources, inspiration, ideas for projects, and tips for how to begin. Then begin your own story. What problem will your class help to solve? Where will interest, motivation, and ideas take your students? How will you help shape our future leaders, by letting them begin to do the real work that is required in a democracy—research, problem solving, communication, and action? The answer is up to you. My hope is that now, after reading this book, the task is less daunting and more exciting and invigorating to your teaching. Let your students change the world, and get ready to show everyone what they have done.

Afterword

It is not always easy to do the right thing in education. As teachers, we know the best ways to teach and reach our students. But with many of the conditions in today's classrooms—chopped-up schedules, standardized testing environments, pressure from parents and administrators, and behavior challenges—it is easier to just do the same type of teaching many of us had as children (lectures and note taking). Or teach the same units we have been teaching for years. We know the value of project- and inquiry-based learning, but the realities of making it happen are much easier said than done.

For today's children, though, service learning and other forms of innovative teaching should be the norm, not the exception. With society's ever increasing challenges, and rapid and instant changes to technology and the way we communicate, we need to be raising critical-thinking, problem-solving, community-minded citizens.

Service learning is one way you can do just that. You might have to fit it in creatively; you might have to integrate it with what you already teach (as described in this book). By doing so, you are honoring what is better for our students—academically, socially, and for the world.

I frequently tell my students not to always take the easy road. For you, a teacher, I encourage the same. Service learning is not easy, but I hope this book has made it more doable and manageable for you. As you proceed with service learning, you will learn invaluable lessons that you can then pass on to other interested teachers. When that happens, teacher by teacher, student by student, we are changing the world.

Appendix

Appendix 2.1
Principal Discussion Guide
Use this guide to convince your principal to support your work in service learning. This can also be easily modified and copied for use with parents.

Service learning

- raises standardized test scores.
- improves attendance.
- develops a sense of civic responsibility.
- improves GPA.
- develops critical thinking skills.
- improves student behavior and positive attitudes.
- promotes a strong school and community connection.
- allows for more parent volunteerism and involvement.
- solves school and community problems.
- is innovative, creative, and integrated learning.
- promotes twenty-first-century learning skills.

For full citations, please see the reference section at the end of this book.

Appendix 3.0
Service-Learning Project Idea List (by Academic Subject)
Teachers: Keep in mind this is a list of service-learning ideas, and not a laundry list of community service projects. To be service learning, it needs to be integrated into your curricular goals and provide for assessment and

reflection of learning. These are just a few ideas per topic. You are sure to think of more, and you will find more ideas sprinkled throughout this book. These ideas can be adapted to any grade level.

Science and Health

- Lake, pond, river, or stream assessment and action (cleanup, legislation, park development, preservation of habitat, invasive species removal, biodiversity study, species assessment, species study and conservation, etc.).
- Local habitat preservation (teams assess, sign, and teach about a local habitat). This could be any habitat.
- Local species preservation (teams discover local species in need, work to protect them, and teach others). This could be any species.
- A disease or condition of the human body present in the local community (students learn about it, interview health care providers and experts, then teach the school community about it).
- Local geological areas of interest (learn about the area's geologic history, develop a community resource, and teach about it).
- Study how robotics are used in our society—for example, to aid construction, people with disabilities, or in industry—create a prototype of similar design, and share with the school community.
- Human body tests to promote fitness (students could develop health and fitness tests for the school community, then communicate results and how to improve for better fitness).
- Create a picture book about a science theme. Share this with a lower grade level.

Language Arts, English, and Literacy

- Interview local authors, create a community resource, and share it with the school community.
- Interview community elders, create a community resource or project, and share it with the school community.
- Create films about your school's literacy program. Edit, finalize, and share it with the school community.
- Create plays in the style of a studied author or within a theme. Perform for the school.
- Create a newspaper or magazine for your community, with all the parts. Find community funding and share.

Math

- Hold a math night for the community. Students plan all the details within a curricular theme.

- Create a picture book about math themes and concepts to share with the lower grades.
- Interest lower grades in math. Hold a math fair and develop high-interest activities to lead.
- Interview local professionals who use math in their jobs. Create a community resource (book, website, guide, etc.) and share.
- Develop a web quest or online tutorial for a math concept or concepts to share.
- Create a series of math games (in a curricular area assigned) for your grade level and share.

Social Studies

- Develop a play, book, or website to communicate a period of time and share with the community.
- Create a song, poem, or puppet show to teach about an historical figure, important event, or time period.
- Hold a history fair within a curricular theme. Students study their historical person fully, dress up in character, and talk with the school community at the fair.
- Create new legislation to solve a community problem. Take it to the local legislator or the capitol of your state to share.
- Interview local politicians about a topic tied to your curricular goals. Create a way to share these interviews (movie, website, play, poem, newspaper, etc.).

Music

- Create musical instruments from reused and recycled materials. Teach the younger grades about how to play them, then donate them to a class.
- Create a musical score to describe something: a season, a feeling, or a curricular theme. Then share with the school.
- Interview local musicians about a theme or curricular goal in music. Then share with the school community what you have learned.
- Write songs to share about a theme in music class. Share with the school community.

Art

- Find a community need for art: a mural in an alley, hospital or clinic, rundown area of town, or on the side of the school. Work together to create it.

- Find someone in the community in need. Create art for that person based on their interests and present it to him or her in a community event.
- Create an art show for an approved charity. Create art to sell in an evening community event to raise funds for the charity (or your school).
- Teach the lower grades about an art concept, famous artist, or period of time in art. Discover a creative way to teach them about it.

Physical Education

- Interview the staff of a school about their exercise habits. Create a movie, book, or website to share with the school community.
- Hold a school wide fitness or wellness event. Students plan and coordinate the whole event with teacher support.

Appendix 3.1
Sample Parent Letter

Dear Parents and Guardians,

I am currently planning an exciting new multidisciplinary unit of study. The Vermont Standards call for the sciences to be connected and integrated. This unit will do just that. Our focus will be on the natural and cultural history of the Worcester Mountain Range and its watershed.

Our approach will be through Service Learning. Service Learning is a "method of teaching and learning that challenges students to identify research, propose, and implement solutions to real needs in their school or community" (KIDS Consortium, 2001). Our district has expressed interest in incorporating Service Learning into its curriculum, and it has been included in our Action Plan.

Our unit on the Worcester Mountain Watershed will utilize resources in our own community. Student research will add to our community's awareness of our local natural resources.

With clear teacher guidance, Service Learning allows students to drive the course of study and action. I will provide instruction, along with community volunteers and experts, as well as resources and connections to facilitate projects that students select. Students will have a Celebrate the Worcester Watershed Community Day where they share their work with the school and greater community. Specific science instruction during this unit may take the form of aquatic or forest ecology, as well as other sciences. Additionally, student groups may branch into other ideas. There will be a portfolio for assessment that students will complete, with expectations clearly outlined. I will send home a copy of this portfolio for you to look at with your child. Please also see the attached Vermont Standards I feel will be addressed by this unit.

Please consider volunteering to help us with this project. Any time you can give would be helpful, and I have many ideas for ways that you can support our work. Please call or e-mail me, or send in a note of interest with your child, and I will get back to you with specific ways that you can volunteer.

Please feel free to call with questions or concerns. I feel this is an exciting opportunity for our fifth- and sixth-grade students, and I hope you do too!

Sincerely,

Katy Farber, 5/6 Teacher, Rumney School

5/6 Wonders of the Worcester Watershed Unit
Vermont Standards Linking

Students in our 5/6 unit will have the opportunity to meet several of the Vermont Standards throughout their study. Some standards will be focused on more than others as a result of the topic of study. Listed below are the standards I believe will be met throughout this unit.

The Vital Results are personal development standards that cut across all fields of knowledge. This unit will involve students working on their projects in small groups, which will provide many opportunities for growth in the area of the Vital Results.

The areas of the Vital Results that this unit will address are: Communication, Reasoning and Problem Solving, Personal Development, and Civic/Social Responsibility.

Communication: Students will need to research their topic idea using technology, reading in content areas, listening to presentations, writing for an authentic purpose, and using presentation skills.

Reasoning and Problem Solving: Students will ask guiding questions, select a focus, and think creatively.

Personal Development: Students will have choices in this project, which will help them develop a sense of personal competence. They will have to make informed, educated decisions and work collaboratively within a student team.

Civic/Social Responsibility: Students will gain an understanding of community values and democratic processes, and learn by serving our Middlesex community information about the Worcester Mountain watershed area.

Fields of Knowledge

Geography

Geographical Knowledge

Standard 6.7: Students use geographical knowledge and images of various places to understand the present, communicate historical interpretations, develop solutions for problems, and plan for the future.

Curricular goal: Students in this unit will use mapping skills, strive to learn the physical and cultural geography of our area, analyze land use problems, and research how geography influences our communities.

Interrelationships

Standard 6.9: Students examine the interrelationships among physical earth processes, ecosystems, and human activities.

Curricular goal: Students in this unit will locate and describe various ecosystems in Vermont, demonstrate how human actions can modify the environment, and examine the interrelationships between earth's ecosystems.

Inquiry, Experimentation, and Theory

Scientific Method

Standard 7.1: Students use scientific methods to describe, investigate, and explain phenomena.

Curricular goal: Students in this unit may choose to design an experiment that uses the scientific method.

Standard 7.2: Students design and conduct a variety of their own investigations and projects.

Curricular goal: Students in this service-learning project will be designing and conducting their own research project and presentation.

Systems

Analysis

Standard 7.11: Students analyze and understand living and non-living systems as collections of interrelated parts and interconnected systems.

Curricular goal: Students will demonstrate throughout this unit an understanding that systems are connected and how one affects how others work.

The Living World

Organisms, Evolution, and Interdependence

Standard 7.13: Students understand the characteristics of organisms, see patterns of similarity and differences among living organisms, understand the role of evolution, and recognize the interdependence of all systems that support life.

Curricular goal: Students in this unit will investigate the interdependence of all systems that support life (water cycle, food chains, populations).

Appendix 3.2
Bloom's Thinking Taxonomy (1956)
Level 1
Knowledge-Recall
Verbs: tell, list, describe, name, locate

Level 2
Comprehension-Understanding
Verbs: restate, outline, predict
Level 3
Application-Transfer
Verbs: show, solve, use, illustrate, examine, classify
Level 4
Analysis-Examining
Verbs: analyze, investigate, compare and contrast, distinguish
Level 5
Synthesis-Combining
Verbs: create, invent, construct, design, compose, plan, imagine
Level 6
Evaluation-Rating
Verbs: judge, select, choose, debate, justify, recommend, assess

Appendix 3.3
Wonders of the Worcester Watershed Guiding Questions
Background information: Our school sits in the Worcester Mountain Range. We see the mountains outside of our school every day. Many of your homes are in and around the mountains. What is a watershed? Many of you studied this concept in science last year. A watershed (also called a drainage basin) is land area from which a river and all its tributaries get their water.

During this brainstorm you will think about what you want to know about this unique community in which we live. During this unit, as we discussed in the introduction, you will get to research a subject you are interested in and create some way to share your information with the Middlesex community.

To help you get started in generating ideas, take a look at some of the materials set out in your classroom. There are some books, maps, and pictures to help you.

Then independently answer the following questions. After that, you will share your answers with a small group, then with the whole class. This will help us understand your areas of interest.

1. What do you want to investigate about our local mountains and watershed?
2. What do you recommend or imagine Middlesex community members should know about the Worcester mountains and watershed?
3. What are you curious about in our area? What have you always wanted to learn more about but have never had the chance? Create two or three

questions about anything you would like to learn more about within our local mountains and watershed. (Please write your answers in a question format.)

Appendix 3.4
Wonders of the Worcester Watershed
Master Question List
Student directions: These are all of your responses to the guided questions. Read through the questions below. They are broken into areas of interest. Please number your preference for a project topic from one to five (one being your first choice, five being your last). Put the number clearly to the right of the chosen question.
Thanks!
   WW = Worcester Watershed

Physical Science
   1. What are the water sources of the WW and why is it called that?
   2. How did the WW form?
   3. Where does the most water flow in the WW and where does it start and end?
   4. What and where are the different tributaries (streams and rivers) coming off of Hunger Mountain?
   5. How does the WW work?
   6. Why is the top of Hunger Mountain bald?
   7. How has the mountain environment changed over the years?
   8. How has the weather affected the WW over time and have there been any major storms in history?
   9. Has Vermont ever had an earthquake? When, where, and why?
   10. What would a map or model of the entire WW look like?
   11. What is the geological history of the WW?
   12. Have there been fires or floods in the WW? If so, when and what were the effects?
   13. What mapping skills would help you travel on foot in the WW?
   14. What soil type is found in the WW and what can be learned about it?
   15. What mountains and communities make up the WW?

Life Science
   1. Are there still wolves in Vermont? What is the history of sightings and predictions?
   2. What is the most common animal in the WW and what can be learned about it?

3. What is the history of bears in the WW?
4. Why are there so many fishers?
5. What animals were here in history that aren't anymore? What happened and why?
6. What reptiles live here and how do they develop?
7. Are there any endangered species that live in the WW? What are they and what is their status?
8. What plants are dangerous that live here?
9. What hawks live in the WW and what can I learn about them?
10. What lives in the swamps, marshes, and wetlands, and where are they located in the WW?
11. What turtles live in the WW and how do they sound, eat, and function?
12. Are bobcats going extinct? What can be learned about their current population?
13. When was the last mountain lion seen and are there any left?
14. What kind of insects live in the WW?
15. Where do frogs live in the WW? What species are there? What do they eat? How do roads affect them?
16. What animal habitats are in the WW?
17. What tracks go with what animal? What can they tell us?
18. What fish live in ponds, rivers, and streams in the WW?
19. What is the biology of raccoons?

Social
1. What are the legends, history, and stories of the WW?
2. Who were some of the first people here?
3. Who discovered Hunger Mountain? What was their story?
4. How long has Hunger Mountain been named and was it called something else at one point?
5. Have people in the past ever lived on Hunger Mountain?
6. Why are there stone walls in the woods? What can we learn from them?
7. What is the highest population of the WW and what are the impacts on our area?
8. What plants are/were used to cure illnesses?
9. What do you do if you run into a wild animal?
10. What minerals can be found in the WW? Is there any gold?
11. What are good wilderness skills for surviving in the mountains?

Human Impact
1. How does pollution travel and affect the WW?
2. How do we decide what a good use of our land is in the WW?

3. How do humans affect the ecosystems of WW?
4. What does it mean to be an ethical hunter?
5. How clean is our water?
6. What trails are in this area and where are they accessed?
7. Is there pollution in our rivers and how is it affecting the WW?
8. Is global warming affecting our snow totals? What can be learned about this?

Appendix 4.1
Planning Checklist
(The concepts below are outlined more fully in chapter 4.)
✓ Decide on the length of the unit.
✓ Schedule the culminating event (learning fair or festival).
✓ Meet with your teaching team.
✓ Meet with your principal.
✓ Share about your project with the school staff.
✓ Plan your assessment for the unit.
✓ Brainstorm your needed resources.
✓ Get organized (binder or system for all the project materials).
✓ Plan for the culminating event (where, when, who will be invited, publicize).
✓ Plan for preteaching

Appendix 5.1
Contact Log
Enter in the names, jobs, and contact information for everyone you contact regarding the project.

Person contacted	Role or job	Type of contact (e-mail, phone call, interview, letter)	Date

Appendix 5.2
Parent Survey
Dear Parents and Guardians,
Please take a moment to tell me a little about your profession, interests, hobbies, and your potential interest in volunteering in your child's classroom. It is very important for children to be exposed to as many role models as possible, and your involvement over the next year would enrich our studies and connections to the community. Thanks for your time!

Name: _____

Job: _____

Hobbies: _____

Sports interests: _____

Special skills and interests: _____

Would you be willing to share about any of the above topics with our class?

_____

Would you be willing to do a presentation about your job?

_____

Would you be willing to volunteer to help with our service-learning projects?

_____

Please list any other way you might be involved in volunteering this year (field trip chaperone, student assistance, room parent and organizer, or any other ideas!).

_____

Thank you.

Appendix 5.3
Sample Press Release
Headline Is in Title Case Meaning You Capitalize Every Word Except for Prepositions and Articles of Three Words or Less and Short; Ideally it is Not More Than 170 Characters and Does Not Take a Period

The summary paragraph is a synopsis of the press release in regular sentence form. It does not merely repeat the headline or opening paragraph: it tells the story in a different way. The summary paragraph is mandatory at Free Press Release Center.

City, State (FPRC) Month 1, 2005—The first paragraph, know as the lead, contains the most important information. You need to grab your reader's attention here. And you cannot assume that they have read the headline or summary paragraph; the lead should stand on its own.

A press release, like a news story, keeps sentences and paragraphs short, about three or four lines per paragraph. The first couple of paragraphs should cover the who, what, when, where, why, and how questions.

The rest of the news release expounds on the information provided in the lead paragraph. It includes quotes from key staff, customers, or subject matter experts. It contains more details about the news you have to tell, which can be about something unique or controversial or about a prominent person, place, or thing.

"You should include a quote for that human touch," said Gary Sims, CEO of the Free Press Release Center. "And you should use the last paragraph to restate and summarize the key points."

This is a sample press release template for use at the Free Press Release Center. The last paragraph can also include details on product availability, trademark acknowledgments, and so forth.

About ABC Company:

Include a short corporate backgrounder about the company or the person who is newsworthy before you list the contact person's name and phone number.

Contact:
name
title
phone number
e-mail or web address
Source: Free Press Release Center

Appendix 5.4
Press Release Sample
Math Rocks! Students Give Math an Image Makeover
Math is underrated and often students who like it are stereotyped, and the students of Centre Hall School are taking this message to the community.

Ms. Bevin's seventh-grade math classes have been creating a math fair to showcase how cool math can be. In groups of three or four, these students have created projects to showcase their math skills and lift the profile of this subject.

State College, Pennsylvania, May 23, 2010—At Centre Hall School, students in the seventh grade took over the gym to showcase their cool math skills. As part of a service-learning project led by Ms. Bevin, seventh-grade math teacher, students set up stations and demonstrated their math skills to the entire middle-school community. At one station, students lined up to take free throw shots at the basketball hoop, and students taught each other how to calculate their own sports stats using fractions, decimals, and percents. At another station, tessellation art was hung on the walls and students showed small groups how to create them. This project is part of a schoolwide effort to make math come alive for students and to connect it to real life.

Ms. Bevin was clearly proud of her students. She said, "Math doesn't have to be sedentary or boring. These students are making it come alive for everyone— and showing each other that they can enjoy learning and teaching math."

Principal Phil Bosco agreed. "I grew up doing math alone, at my desk, in isolation. I didn't enjoy it very much. I wish I had Ms. Bevin back in seventh grade. I think this kind of hands on learning will empower some of our students to see themselves as mathematicians—and possibly have a future in this area."

About Ms. Bevins:

Ms. Bevins is in her fourth year teaching at Centre Hall School and believes service-learning projects like this motivate and inspire her students.

Contact:
Ms. Bevins, Seventh-Grade Math Teacher at Centre Hall School
888-888-8888

Appendix 7.1
Student Portfolio Cover Sheet

Name _____

Teacher directions: Students can keep this portfolio in a binder or folder for the length of the project.

Please make sure all the items listed below are present and in this order. Check when completed. The blank lines at the end of the list are for you to include different assessments particular to your project.

Table of Contents

_____ brainstorming web

_____ planning sheet

_____ timeline

_____ content area reading

_____ five journal entries (dated)

_____ project notes and information

     _____ vocabulary list

     _____ supporting questions

     _____ big ideas and questions

     _____ presentation notes

     _____ research/information

     _____ diagrams, drawings, and charts

_____ self-assessments

     _____ weekly self-assessments

     _____ weekly group assessments

     _____ unit teamwork rubric

     _____ project rubric

_____ _____

_____ _____

Appendix 7.2
Brainstorming Web
Student Directions: Put your guiding question or topic in the center. List any and all ideas about what to do for your service-learning project. Remember to include written and visual ways to share information, and be creative!

Figure A7.2

Appendix 7.3
Timeline for Service-Learning Project

Person	Task (job)	Due date	Notes	Check when complete

Overall Project Due Date: _____

Service-Learning Festival: _____

Appendix 7.4
Student Planning Sheet—Service-Learning Project
Focus Question or Topic Area:

Directions: Please describe the project you plan on completing with your group. It needs to have visual and written components. See the project rubric for the requirements. These can be combined into one project, but the parts need to be completed and handed in.

Visual (a way of communicating your information visually to the audience):

Written (script, report, story, etc. communicating information about your topic area):

Materials you think you will need:

How will your project help the community?

Appendix 7.5
Content Area Reading
Directions: When you get a source that has information—from the Internet, a book, magazine, or newspaper—be sure to write down the information here to keep track of your work. Try to have at least five different sources (not all Internet!)

Type of source	Title	Author	Page numbers or website address

Appendix 7.6
Vocabulary List

Directions: Write down the new vocabulary you learned in your research. You will be expected to list and define at least 10 words and thoroughly understand their meaning.

Word	Meaning

Appendix 7.7
Supporting Questions
Directions: As you come up with more detailed and focused questions during your research, please write them down on this sheet. Put a check next to questions your group is able to answer during this project. You can show your answers in several ways—in your project's written or visual component, or orally during the presentation. Have a goal of 10 questions—with at least 8 answered!

Question	Answered?

Appendix 7.8
Big Ideas and Questions

Directions for students: As you complete your research and work on your project, list any questions here that you want to know the answer to. Think big! It does not have to relate to your topic. It is wide open, just like your mind.

Questions:

1.

2.

3.

4.

5.

6.

7.

8.

These questions might lead you to some big ideas about the world. What do you think should happen next? What would you do if you could? How should the world change? What difference do you want to make?

1.

2.

3.

4.

5.

Appendix 7.9
Service-Learning Project Rubric

	1 (limited work shared)	2 (does not meet standards)	3 (close to meeting standards)	4 (meeting standards)
Visual	Limited visual presented.	Visual is partially completed, or not very clear, colorful, or detailed; communicated some learned information, but it is not organized.	Visual is complete; showing detail, color, and clear information; some aspect of the visual has problem(s) with clarity and/or understanding.	Visual is complete, organized, clear, and detailed; communicates learned information in a creative and understandable way.
Written	Limited written piece shared.	Partially complete, lacks details or focus, or is in rough draft form with errors; communicates some information learned in the research process.	Complete in final draft form and shows an understanding of the information learned in the research process; some problems with the piece are evident.	Complete in final draft form and shows a thorough understanding of the information learned in the research process; is interesting and engaging to the reader.

(Continued...)

	1 (limited work shared)	2 (does not meet standards)	3 (close to meeting standards)	4 (meeting standards)
Presentation	Student did not have a role in the presentation.	Student had a limited role in the presentation.	Student had a role in the presentation; used some good speaking skills, and shared information.	Student had well-rehearsed role in the presentation; used good speaking skills and shared information enthusiastically with the school community.

** To achieve a 5, a student needs to show exceptional effort in the visual, written, and presentation portions of this project. This will be evident from the quality in each area. Extending the project beyond standards can include more depth of study, a creative and unique approach to the project's written and visual components, and an outstanding and creative presentation.

Appendix 7.10
Weekly Journal
Teachers: Assign a specific length for the journal entry based on the age of the students you work with.

Name _____

Directions: During the unit, please reflect weekly about your project. You can write about lots of thoughts regarding your service-learning project. Some ideas:

- What you have learned and connections to your new knowledge.
- Describe your experiences with your group as you discover new information.
- Describe a hands-on experience within this project.
- Explain what this project makes you think about.
- Your concerns, thoughts, and ideas about how to solve a problem you discovered.
- Describe your feelings about your group, topic area, or the project in general.

Appendix 7.11
Teamwork Rubric (Student self-assesses in pencil, hands it in, and the teacher assesses in pen.)

	1 (limited teamwork demonstrated)	2 (does not meet standards)	3 (close to meeting standards)	4 (meets the standard)	5 (exceeds the standard)
Research and Gather Information	Does not collect any information that relates to the topic.	Collects very little information, some relates to the topic.	Collects some basic information, most relates to the topic.	Collects a great deal of information, all relates to the topic.	Collects a great deal of information, all relates to the topic; helps others in the research process.
Share Information	Does not relay any information to teammates.	Relays very little information, some relates to the topic.	Relays some basic information, most relates to the topic.	Relays a great deal of information, all relates to the topic.	Relays a great deal of information, goes beyond what is expected.
Be Punctual	Does not hand in any assignments.	Hands in most assignments late.	Hands in assignments some of the time.	Hands in assignments most of the time.	Hands in all assignments on time.
Fulfill Team Duties	Does not perform any duties of assigned team role.	Performs very little duties.	Performs nearly all duties.	Performs all duties of assigned team role.	Performs all duties of assigned team role and goes above and beyond that role.
Share Equally	Always relies on others to do the work.	Rarely does the assigned work—often needs reminding.	Usually does the assigned work—sometimes needs reminding.	Does the assigned work with very little reminding.	Always does the assigned work without having to be reminded.

Used with permission of Community Works Institute. www.communityworksinstitute.org.

Appendix 7.12
Weekly Self-Assessment

Students: Complete the self-assessment assignment every week during the project.

Name _____

Directions: Please answer the following questions in at least two sentences each.

1. How was my participation and motivation this week in my group?

2. What did I do well this week and what were some of my challenges?

3. What can I do next week to improve?

Weekly Group Assessment

Students: All students complete this weekly group assessment every week of the project. Do this independently.

1. How did my group members do with participation and motivation this week?

2. What were some of the things my group did well and what were some of the challenges?

3. What can my group do next week to improve?

Appendix 8.1
Small-Group Reflection Questions

- How is this group working together?
- What has been challenging?
- What has been going well, and why do you think that is?
- What has changed from your original plan?
- What has surprised you about your work?
- What questions has your work made you think of?
- How does your project connect with others?
- How can your group members work more effectively with one another?
- What skills have you been using? What ones would you like to use?

Appendix 8.2
Whole Class Reflection Questions

- Have each group share about their projects and work.
- Have students do a whip-around (each class member shares briefly) about one interesting fact from their research.
- Ask students to say what has surprised them.
- Ask students what skills they have been using in their work, and how they could improve or expand them.
- Ask students to make connections to projects and other areas in academics or in life.
- Ask students if they could wave a magic wand and change something, what would it be?

References

Billig, S. (2002). Using Evidence to Make the Case for Service-Learning as an Academic Achievement Intervention in K–12 Schools. Retrieved March 29, 2010, from http://www.seanetonline.org/images/UsingEvidencetoMaketheCasefor Service.doc.

———. (n.d.). Using Evidence to Make the Case for Service-Learning as an Academic Achievement Intervention in K–12 Schools. RMC Research Corporation. Retrieved March 20, 2010, from http://74.125.93.132/search? q=cache:Y6rUlJ41wj0J:www.service-learningpartnership.org/site/DocServer/ caseforsl.doc%3FdocID%3D106+www.seanetonline.org/images/UsingEvidenceto MaketheCaseforService.doc+service+learning+and+standardized+testing&cd=1& hl=en&ct=clnk&gl=us.

Brenner, J. (2010). Observations on Effective Teams: "Working Together Works." Concurrent Session Team Development and Tuckman's Model—In Brief. Retrieved July 19, 2010, from http://webcache.googleusercontent.com/ search?q=cache:siTIEoF4F-QJ:groups.ucanr.org/ANR_Leadership/files/25753.doc+ tuckman's+stages+of+teamwork+model&cd=6&hl=en&ct=clnk&gl=us&client= safari.

Bridgeland, J., DiIulio, J., and Wulsin, S. (2008). Engaged for Success: Service Learning as a Tool for Dropout Prevention. Civic Enterprises. Retrieved March 27, 2010, from http://docs.google.com/viewer?a=v&q=cache:Kf5pFlftonQJ:www. civicenterprises.net/pdfs/service-learning.pdf+http://www.civicenterprises.net/ pdfs/service-learning.pdf&hl=en&gl=us&pid=bl&srcid=ADGEESiDstise8PZ7 pYintaU5GbqmdGrSLgotHRnZKpTrrODebk4bulSaR3LxEl4bLG5Xf51 GFVONZVKr9NqHJ7BwfyuF8DQX-HScTker6EkWc9SgOe5HM3UElXb- S3NKN3Z39K6cHaYd&sig=AHIEtbQM_qgYUJ_B8-0bkqCQh0BoK50w0A.

Bridgeland, J., DiIulio, J., Jr., and Morison, K. (2006). The Silent Epidemic: Perspectives of High School Dropouts. Retrieved March 29, 2010, from http://www. civicenterprises.net/pdfs/thesilentepidemic3-06.pdf.

Community Works Institute. Service Learning and Assessment: A Field Guide for Teachers. Retrieved May 2, 2010, from http://www.communityworksinstitute.org/cwpublications/slassessguide/slassessguide.html.

Curtis, D. (2001). Real World Issues Motivate Students. *Edutopia.* Retrieved March 29, 2010, from http://www.edutopia.org/start-pyramid.

David, J. (2009). Service Learning and Civic Participation. Association for Supervision and Curriculum Development. Retrieved April 24, 2010, from http://www.ascd.org/publications/educational_leadership/may09/vol66/num08/Service_Learning_and_Civic_Participation.aspx.

Eyler, J., and D. E. Giles, J. (1999). *Where's the Learning in Service-Learning?* San Francisco: Jossey-Bass.

Free Press Release Center. (n.d.). Sample Press Release. Retrieved April 24, 2010, from http://www.free-press-release-center.info/sample-press-release.html.

Greenfield, J. (n.d.). Bringing Justice Home: First Steps Towards Community Action. Retrieved April 24, 2010, from http://bostonteachnet.org/greenfield/sigproj.htm.

Hopkins, D. (2008). Is Community Service a Waste of Time? *Education World.* Retrieved April 24, 2010, from http://www.educationworld.com/a_curr/curr188.shtml.

Kahne, J., and Sporte, S. (2007). Developing Citizens: The Impact of Civic Learning Opportunities on Students' Commitment to Civic Participation. Consortium on Chicago School Research. Retrieved March 29, 2010, from http://www.eric.ed.gov/ERICWebPortal/custom/portlets/recordDetails/detailmini.jsp?_nfpb=true&_&ERICExtSearch_SearchValue_0=ED499374&ERICExtSearch_SearchType_0=no&accno=ED499374.

KIDS Consortium. (2005). *Kids as Planners: A Guide to Strengthening Students, Schools, and Communities Through Service-Learning* (second edition). Augurn, ME: KIDS Consortium.

Kohn, A. (2002). Standardized Testing: Separating Wheat Children from Chaff Children. Excerpted from the Foreword to Susan Ohanian's book *What Happened to Recess and Why Are Our Children Struggling in Kindergarten?* New York: McGraw-Hill.

Managing Groups. (n.d.). Teaching Effectiveness Program Academic Learning Service. University of Oregon. Retrieved from http://www.uoregon.edu/~tep/technology/blackboard/docs/groups.pdf on June 23, 2010.

Morgan, W. (1999). Standardized Test Scores Improve with Service Learning. Center for Participation and Citizenship at Indiana University, Bloomington. Retrieved March 20, 2010, from http://www.ri.net/middletown/mef/linksresources/documents/ServiceLearningBetterScores.pdf.

National Center for Education Statistics. (2010). Service-Learning and Community Service in K–12 Public Schools. Retrieved March 20, 2010, from http://nces.ed.gov/surveys/frss/publications/1999043.

National Center for Education Statistics. (1999). Fast Response Survey System, National Student Service-Learning and Community Service Survey. Retrieved March 20, 2010, from http://nces.ed.gov/quicktables/Detail.asp?Key=202.

National Commission on Service Learning. (2010). Learning in Deed, the Power of Service Learning for America's Schools. Retrieved March 20, 2010, from http://nslp.convio.net/site/DocServer/executive_summary.pdf?docID=1202.

National Service Learning Clearinghouse. (2010). What is Service Learning? Retrieved March 20, 2010, from http://www.servicelearning.org/what-service-learning.

National Service Learning Clearinghouse. (2008). Why Districts, Schools and Classrooms Should Practice Service Learning. Retrieved March 20, 2010, from http://www.servicelearning.org/filemanager/download/two-page_fs/Why_Districts,_Schools,_and_Classrooms_Should_Practice_SL_FS_Short_Final_Mar08.pdf.

Pennsylvania Service Learning Alliance. (2002–2007). Reflection: It's Easier Than you Think. Retrieved May 5, 2010, from http://www.paservicelearning.org/Project_Ideas/Reflection.html.

Smink, J., and Reimer, M. (2005). Fifteen Strategies to Improve Attendance and Truancy Prevention. National Dropout Prevention Center. Retrieved March 27, 2010, from http://www.eric.ed.gov/ERICDocs/data/ericdocs2sql/content_storage_01/0000019b/80/1b/ac/a5.pdf.

Steinke, P., and Fitch, P. (2007). Assessing Service-Learning. Research and Practice in Assessment. Volume 1, Issue 2, June 2007. Retrieved May 2, 2010, from http://www.virginiaassessment.org/rpa/2/Steinke%20Fitch.pdf.

University of Southern California (2010). History of Service Learning. Retrieved July 25, 2010, from http://college.usc.edu/history-of-service-learning.

Breinigsville, PA USA
11 January 2011
253034BV00004B/3/P